This book is both an authentic look at the POW experience and also an often amusing account of one man's way of coping with a brutal captivity. Leo Thorsness, my friend and fellow alumnus of the Hanoi Hilton, shows why the North Vietnamese may have had our bodies but never controlled our soul.

　　—*Sen. John McCain*

Our nation's Medal of Honor recipients are the ultimate heroes among us, but the members of this elite fraternity have their *own* heroes, and Leo Thorsness is one of them. Taken to the edge of human existence, he came back with his dignity intact. Leo emerged from the darkness of his brutal confinement in Hanoi because he was armed with a keen intellect, unbreakable mental discipline, and the love of family.

Surviving Hell is a story for all those who think life's challenges are unbearable. What happened to Leo seems like too much for any human to bear, yet he survived and thrived—the ultimate revenge on his captors. In this gripping and harrowing book, Thorsness offers timeless lessons on perseverance, mental focus, and old-fashioned patriotism.

　　—*Brian Williams, anchor and managing editor, NBC Nightly*
　　　News; director, Medal of Honor Foundation Board

In business as in life, the essential building blocks of leadership are character, courage, faith, and loyalty. Leo Thorsness tells a riveting story that speaks of these values with eloquence and uncommon humility. The lessons of this book apply to all those who must confront adversity or meet challenging demands by doing the right thing. It is an uplifting and inspiring guide that should be required reading for leaders everywhere.

　　—*Robert J. Stevens, chairman, president, and CEO,*
　　　Lockheed Martin Corporation

In my career as an actor I have had the opportunity to portray a few fictional war heroes. It is my pleasure to know a real war hero, Leo Thorsness. As a Wild Weasel fighter pilot in Vietnam, he was awarded the Medal of Honor for a mission he flew shortly before being shot down. He spent six years in the brutal Hanoi Hilton as a POW. *Surviving Hell* tells it like it was in combat and in prison, but the story is also uplifting and helpful for anyone going through tough times. Leo is a survivor who shows us that, even in hell, we are much stronger than we think.

　　—*Gary Sinise, actor*

For three years I lived in cells with or near Leo Thorsness at the Hanoi Hilton, and I vouch for his account of captivity in that hellhole. It was especially bad for Leo because his back was fractured from torture, which required him to be strung up by the feet to sleep. Yet in our many POW conversations, we were optimistic that we would someday be free and upbeat about how we would use our freedom. The most important thing was to return home with honor; and that, Leo has certainly done.

> —*Col. Bud Day, USAF (ret.); Medal of Honor recipient; fellow POW with Leo Thorsness; author of* Return With Honor

In a brisk and vivid style, Leo Thorsness transports us into the darkness of the POW's world without ever succumbing to despair. His story is a saga of uncommon valor, told with humility and good humor.

I first met this extraordinary American hero—who cleverly disguises himself as "just another guy"—on the set of *The Hanoi Hilton*, where he served as my technical advisor and became my friend. To watch Leo relive his experiences with those who would portray him and his comrades-in-arms was an inspiration to us all. Now, in *Surviving Hell*, he makes that journey accessible to everyone in a way that brings hope.

Freedom is certainly not free, and here's a chance to understand why some people are willing to pay the price, yet never lose their humanity.

> —*Lionel Chetwynd, filmmaker; Oscar and Emmy nominee; writer and director of* The Hanoi Hilton

How can a simple man have so much to say to every reader? Leo Thorsness grew up "average," as he says, but then decided to serve our country in the Air Force, a commitment that led him into the horrors of a North Vietnam prison. His story will inspire you to do more. This book conveys the message that Leo has been taking to corporate executives, "Do What's Right—Help Others (DWR-HO)," and the lesson he teaches America's children about the "4 F's: Faith, Family, Friends, Fun." *Surviving Hell* shows how to frame your life for the better, regardless of the hand you've been dealt. Leo did it; you can too!

> —*Tom Matthews, president, Medal of Honor Foundation; former president and CEO, Smith Barney Global Private Client Division*

The human spirit is amazingly resilient! In this incredible story of one man's deliverance from "hell on earth," Leo Thorsness shows that he truly understands these words from the Bible: "The Lord is my light and my salvation—whom shall I fear? The Lord is the stronghold of my life—of whom shall I be afraid?" Your heart will be stirred to sadness, then anger, then despair, and finally to hope as the journey home for Leo becomes a reality. This is an astounding account of God's faithfulness to one man.
> —Rev. Dale Seley, pastor, Downtown Baptist Church,
> Alexandria, Virginia

It is my high honor and privilege to be a close friend of the Thorsness family. Leo is a genuine hero who always demonstrates his love for America. *Surviving Hell: A POW's Journey* is a reminder that freedom isn't free, and an enduring tribute to those who made supreme sacrifices under the most intolerable conditions. After reading this book, you will never again think you are having a bad day.
> —Bruce N. Whitman, president and CEO,
> FlightSafety International

One never knows the tests that the road of life will bring, but *Surviving Hell* demonstrates that the virtues of honor, courage, sacrifice— undergirded by an unshakable faith and the love of family—enable one to triumph even in the most unthinkable circumstances. As one who is privileged to know Col. Leo Thorsness and his wife, Gaylee, I am grateful for their willingness to share this story so that it may provide a beacon of hope and a guidebook for the rest of us on our life's journey.
> —David McIntyre, president and CEO,
> TriWest Healthcare Alliance

I first met Leo Thorsness at Spangdahlem, Germany, in 1960; but I really got to know him when I wrote the recommendation for his Medal of Honor in 1967. Leo is unique in combining the skills of an expert fighter pilot with a keen analytical ability. He developed tactics that allowed the Wild Weasels to accomplish our mission in North Vietnam and reduced our losses by over 50 percent. No one single person did more for those who flew to Hanoi. The United States Air Force owes Leo a huge debt, and I am personally in his debt because he gave me the tools to survive my forty-seven trips to Hanoi.
> —Lt. Col. Billy R. Sparks, USAF (ret.)

Leo was the boss of our Wild Weasel SAM hunters, and if he was on our daily trip to Hanoi, it was no sweat. I saw him being shot down, and as I set up the rescue attempt and talked to him on his fragile survival radio, the last thing he said to me was "Get me out of here!" We could not, and thus began this remarkable story of skill, heroism, and bravery.

—*Col. Jack Broughton, USAF (ret.)*

Leo Thorsness describes the combat mission of a lifetime, which would earn him our nation's highest award for valor, the Medal of Honor. But the exhilaration of aerial victories over enemy MiGs and coaxing the last measure of performance out of his fuel-thirsty "Thud" was followed in an instant by a low-tech experience that would deprive him of his freedom for six years. Thorsness will make you cry and make you laugh as he describes the highs and lows of his extended visit to a hell that most of us can hardly imagine. It would change his life forever.

—*Lt. Gen. Nick Kehoe, USAF (ret.); president,*
Medal of Honor Foundation

I came away . . . with renewed gratitude for our freedom, but also especially for great-souled men such as Thorsness. The sacrifices of such men, it cannot be recalled often enough, make us the land of the free because we're also the home of the brave.

—*Power Line Blog: John Hinderaker, Scott Johnson,*
Paul Mirengoff

SURVIVING HELL
A POW's JOURNEY

SURVIVING HELL

A POW's JOURNEY

LEO THORSNESS

ENCOUNTER BOOKS

New York   London

First American edition published in 2008 by Encounter Books,
    an activity of Encounter for Culture and Education, Inc.,
    a nonprofit, tax exempt corporation.

Encounter Books website address: www.encounterbooks.com

Manufactured in the United States and printed on acid-free paper.
    The paper used in this publication meets the minimum requirements
    of ANSI/NISO Z39.48–1992 (R 1997) (Permanence of Paper).

PAPERBACK EDITION ISBN 978-1-59403-520-3

THE LIBRARY OF CONGRESS HAS CATALOGUED
THE HARDCOVER EDITION AS FOLLOWS:

Thorsness, Leo (Leo K.), 1932-
    Surviving hell : a POW's journey / Leo Thorsness. — 1st hardcover ed.
       p. cm.
    Includes index.
    ISBN-13: 978-1-59403-236-3 (hardcover : alk. paper)
    ISBN-10: 1-59403-236-X (hardcover : alk. paper) 1. Thorsness, Leo
(Leo K.), 1932- 2. Vietnam War, 1961-1975—Prisoners and prisons,
North Vietnamese. 3. Vietnam War, 1961-1975—Personal narratives,
American. 4. Prisoners of war—United States—Biography.
5. Prisoners of war—Vietnam—Biography. 6. Fighter pilots—
United States—Biography. I. Title.
    DS559.4.T49 2008
    959.704'37—dc22
    [B]

                                                          2008002997

Gaylee, you are the love of my life. Thank you for your
intelligence, grit, support, loyalty, beauty, and humor;
for being my best friend; and for filling in as both mom
and dad for our daughter, Dawn, from age 12 to 18.

Dawn, you turned out so beautiful, so moral, and so bright.
I'll work hard to make up the seven years I missed in
your life.

AUTHOR'S NOTE

My experience in Southeast Asia was often traumatic. For the past 35 years, my mind has worked to process what happened. With the benefit of perspective, I wanted to write an account that would be helpful to people going through tough times. Time heals most things, and we are stronger than we think. I thank all who volunteer to serve in the military. During the swearing in, as you raise your hand pledging allegiance to the United States, you do not know the future: Your service may be anything between a hitch in Hawaii and years as a POW in a Hanoi hellhole.

A day never passes without a thought of one or more of the outstanding Americans I had the privilege of serving with as a POW in the most trying of times. Even harder to think about are the families who never found out about a missing-in-action husband or father or son. For some, it is 40 years, and they are still waiting. Bless you and may you find peace.

The years since prison were worth the wait. America, my family, and my friends have allowed me to be a corporate executive, a state senator, a husband of a wonderful woman for 55 years, the father of an outstanding daughter, and a grandfather of two bright, beautiful little girls. I've retired a couple of times. We have moved several times and found true friends each time. Most importantly, in the 35 years since my release from prison, I've never had a really bad day.

CONTENTS

INTRODUCTION

Sitting in my office in downtown Minneapolis one beautiful summer day in 2008, I received a telephone call from Tom Steward, head of press relations for the office of John McCain's presidential campaign in St. Paul, Minnesota. Tom asked me how I would like to meet a recipient of the Medal of Honor over lunch at the campaign office. I said that sounded great.

Arriving at the McCain office in St. Paul, I was introduced to Leo Thorsness. He was holding a small audience around a table in rapt attention. I vaguely recalled Thorsness as a Vietnam veteran who had narrowly lost a 1974 Senate race to George McGovern in the toxic aftermath of Watergate. That recollection proved accurate, but his record contains a few other items of interest.

He is a native Minnesotan, having been born into a farm family near Walnut Grove, and graduated from Walnut Grove High School in 1950. Walnut Grove is now known only as the home of Laura Ingalls Wilder, author of *Little House on the Prairie*, but it should also be known as the birthplace of the author of *Surviving Hell.*

———

Thorsness left Walnut Grove after high school to attend South Dakota State College, where he met his wife in the freshman registration line. In January 1951 he enlisted in the Air Force, and he graduated from pilot school in 1954. He was a career fighter pilot, reaching the rank of colonel and accumulating 5,000 hours of flying time.

Colonel Thorsness flew 92 and a half Wild Weasel missions over North Vietnam. He earned the Medal of Honor for a Wild Weasel mission he flew on April 19, 1967, eleven days before being shot down. He tells the story of what he calls his Medal of Honor Mission in Chapter 1 of this book, but the Air Force account also makes good reading:

Thorsness, then a major, was "Head Weasel" of the 357th Tactical Fighter Squadron at Takhli Air Base in Thailand. On April 19, 1967, he and his backseater, Capt. Harold Johnson, fought a wild 50-minute duel with SAMs, antiaircraft guns and MiGs. They set out in a formation of four planes. Their target was an army compound near Hanoi, heavily defended. Thorsness directed two of the F-105s north and he and his wingman stayed south, forcing enemy gunners to divide their attention. After initial success at destroying two SAM sites, things turned for the wors[e]. First, Thorsness' wingman was hit by flak. He and his backseater ejected. Then the two Weasels he had sent north were attacked by MiGs. The afterburner of one of the F-105s wouldn't light, so he and his wingman were forced to return to Takhli, leaving Thorsness alone to fight solo.

As the F-105 circled the parachutes, relaying their position to the Search and Rescue Center, Johnson spotted a MiG off their left wing. The F-105, though not designed for air-to-air combat, responded well as Thorsness attacked the MiG and destroyed it with a 20-mm cannon, just as another MiG closed on his tail. Low on fuel, Thorsness broke off the battle and rendezvoused with a tanker.

In the meantime, two A-1E Sandys and a rescue helicopter arrived to look for the crewmen. Upon being advised of that fact, Thorsness, with only 500 rounds of ammunition left, turned back from the tanker to fly cover for the rescue force, knowing there were at least five MiGs in the area. As he approached the area, he spotted four MiG-17 aircraft and initiated an attack on them, damaging one and driving the others away from the rescue scene. His ammunition gone, he returned to the rescue scene, hoping to draw the MiGs away from the remaining A-1E. It could very well have been a suicidal mission, but just as he arrived, so did a U.S. strike force and hit the enemy fighters.

But Thorsness' day wasn't over yet. Again low on fuel, he headed
for a tanker just as one of the strike force pilots, almost out of fuel
himself, radioed him for help. Thorsness knew he couldn't make
Takhli [his home base] without refueling. . . .

Thorsness quickly determined that he might be able to make it
past the Mekong River or even to Udorn Air Base in Thailand,
just across the river. He climbed to 35,000 feet over Laos. Seventy
miles from the river, his fuel gauge showed empty. He throttled to
idle and glided to Udorn; his tanks went dry as he touched down.
By giving up the refueling tanker and directing it to the other
strike fighter, Thorsness saved the pilot from ejecting over Laos.

It is difficult to comprehend that the heroics recognized by
Colonel Thorsness's Medal of Honor were followed by further
displays of heroism approximating the valor he displayed on this
mission. When he was shot down by an air-to-air missile in late
April 1967, he ejected from his exploding fighter doing more than
690 miles per hour, injuring both knees and sustaining multiple
fractures of his back. Like John McCain, he was "tied up" for the
next six years. He was captured and held as a prisoner of war in
the Hanoi Hilton and several other North Vietnamese hellholes,
including the one known as Camp Punishment, reserved for especially "difficult" cases.

His Medal of Honor was awarded in 1969, but was kept a secret
so that the North Vietnamese would not use the citation against
him and aggravate the conditions of his captivity. As it was, he
was tortured unmercifully for his first three years in prison. Upon
his capture, he was tortured in interrogation for 19 days and 18
nights, without sleep.

In my meeting with him, Thorsness mentioned to me in passing (as he writes in this book) that he didn't "break" for 18 days,
after which he finally provided something more than name, rank,
and serial number. As I sat listening to him, I thought to myself, *Someone has to write up this story.* Fortunately, someone has.
Thorsness himself has done so in this moving book.

At 127 pages, *Surviving Hell* is brief and understated. It presents itself as a self-help book. "For the past 35 years," Thorsness writes, "my mind has worked to process what happened." Through the book, he means to make his experience of use to others: "With the benefit of perspective, I wanted to write a book that would be helpful to people going through tough times." For more reasons than one, this book deserves a wide audience.

Thorsness calls the ordeal he endured hell, and no reasonable reader will disagree. Thorsness survived. So can you. He states right up front: "Time heals most things, and we are stronger than we think." Hellish experience lends a certain perspective. "In the 35 years since my release from prison," Thorsness writes, "I've never really had a bad day."

He documents several forms of hell. Regarding the torture he endured upon his capture, for example, he remarks: "I would say that my 18 days and nights of interrogations were unendurable if I hadn't endured." He observes that "[t]here was nothing particularly imaginative about the North Vietnamese techniques. They hadn't improved much on the devices of the Spanish Inquisition." Nevertheless, he relates that he received a sampling of the innovations in torture practiced by a team of three Cubans who had been dispatched to assist the North Vietnamese.

He was distraught when he was broken on day 19 of his initial captivity. "I tried to cry. But I was past tears." Upon his return to his cell, however, he was reassured that everyone who is subjected to such an interrogation "has one of two things happen: either they broke or died—some did both."

The book is divided into short chapters that may alternately elicit tears and laughter. The mistreatment and degradation endured by Thorsness and his fellow prisoners of war—our fellow Americans—are by turns enraging and heartbreaking. At one point Thorsness relates his discovery that the North Vietnamese essentially left those airmen who had lost limbs upon ejection from their aircraft to die. To the North Vietnamese their burden was deemed to outweigh their potential benefit.

When he reached Camp Punishment, Thorsness writes, his

interrogator told him several times: "You must learn to suffer." Thorsness drily records: "This I had already done."

The book is also shot through with the black humor that Thorsness and his fellow prisoners directed at their captivity. The humor played a role of its own in surviving hell. The humor appears regularly throughout the book, but in this connection I especially commend Chapters 13 ("Boredom"), 17 ("The Home Front"), and 18 ("Prison Talk").

Even wives, girlfriends, and the families left behind at home could become the subject of humor. When the prisoners of war finally were allowed to receive brief letters from home, for example, they not only reread them as long as they were allowed to hold onto them, but turned the reading into a group activity. Thorsness recalls from memory the worst-ever letter from home received by one of his fellow prisoners, a particularly tough middle-American farm boy who had survived his original captivity in Laos and deserved better:

> Dear Raymond, this has been a bad year. Hail took our crops—no insurance. Your brother-in-law borrowed your speedboat, hit a rock, it sank. Aunt Clarice died suddenly last August. Dad tipped the tractor but only broke his leg. Your 4-H heifer grew up, became a cow, but she died calving—calf too. We think of you often. Mom and Dad.

"There was dead silence for perhaps a minute," Thorsness relates, as the assembled POWs absorbed the letter:

> Finally, someone said, "Ray, read it again, maybe there's a hidden meaning." He shook his head. After more encouragement, he read it again. When he got to the part "your speedboat sank," a POW in the back could no longer hold his muffled laugh. When Ray read, "she died calving," the snickers turned into open, uncontrolled laughter.
>
> In six years of prison, there was never a more genuine slap-your-thighs, roll-on-your-side laughter. We were in stitches and couldn't stop. Ray, bless him, realized how ridiculous, how totally inappropriate it was for family to write that letter to someone in prison. He joined in the hilarity.

Thorsness ultimately found the resources to "survive hell" in the four F's around which he orients his life: family, faith, fun, and friends. (He gave up a fifth F—flying—as a result of his injuries.) Without expressly highlighting the role of gratitude in helping us come to terms with our personal "tough times," he nevertheless heightens our awareness of it. He reflects, for example:

> In my nearly six years in prison, not a day went by when I didn't think about and hope for freedom. I daydreamed about it, and I night-dreamed about it. I dreamed about it in the indistinct moments that separate sleep and waking. I dreamed about the physical sensation of freedom: how it felt on the body. I dreamed about how freedom might happen: by a daring rescue, by the military defeat of North Vietnam, by a POW exchange.

———

If *Surviving Hell* is in part a self-help manual, it is also a straightforward memoir of Thorsness's captivity as a prisoner of war. As such, it takes its place on the bookshelf alongside such noteworthy memoirs of captivity during the Vietnam War as James N. Rowe's *Five Years to Freedom,* Jeremiah Denton's *When Hell Was In Session,* Robinson Risner's *The Passing of the Night,* Medal of Honor recipient James Stockdale's *In Love and War* (written together with Stockdale's wife, Sybil Stockdale), Medal of Honor recipient George E. "Bud" Day's *Return With Honor,* and John McCain's *Faith of My Fathers* (written with Mark Salter). The title of this book obviously recalls Denton's. As a memoir, this book could also be titled *Remembering Hell.*

Thorsness's book is extraordinarily understated in its remembrance of hard times. Especially when it comes to his own ordeal, much of the suffering is left unstated or implicit in the text. Consider Thorsness's reflection on his first three years in captivity: "It was indescribably difficult surviving the first three years of prison, and, if treatment had not improved, I would not have made it through the next three years."

Thorsness's story is also representative of the stories of those whose service has brought them the Medal of Honor. Thorsness is one of only five living Air Force recipients of the Medal of Honor. He is active with the Medal of Honor Foundation, seeking to convey the stories of living Medal of Honor recipients to a wider audience. One of the foundation's projects was the production of *Medal of Honor: Portraits of Valor Beyond the Call of Duty*, a book that depicts and briefly tells the stories of living Medal of Honor recipients.

The text of *Medal of Honor* was written by the founder and original publisher of Encounter Books, Peter Collier, who donated his services to the project. Collier drew on his experience writing the book for a *Wall Street Journal* column on Memorial Day 2006, called "America's Honor." He noted our inattentiveness to heroes such as Thorsness, and our decreasing ability to understand them. "The notion of sacrifice today provokes puzzlement more often than admiration," Collier explained. "We support the troops, of course, but we also believe that war, being hell, can easily touch them with an evil no cause for engagement can wash away. And in any case we are more comfortable supporting them as victims than as warriors."

One reason we have a hard time understanding men such as Thorsness is their rarity. In this book, Thorsness provides a case study of the "great-souled" or magnanimous man at the summit of human excellence of whom Aristotle speaks in the *Nicomachean Ethics*. If it were not for the example set by men such as Thorsness, we might doubt that such men actually exist.

Aristotle explains (here I am borrowing from the superb translation by Joe Sachs) that the great-souled man is especially concerned with honors and acts of dishonor. The great-souled man, because he holds few things in high honor, is not someone who takes small risks or is passionately devoted to taking risks, but someone who takes great risks. When he does take a risk, he does so without regard for his life, on the ground that it is not just on any terms that life is worth living.

In his Memorial Day column, Collier eloquently explained why we should attend to the story Thorsness exemplifies:

We impoverish ourselves by shunting these heroes and their experiences to the back pages of our national consciousness. Their stories are not just boys' adventure tales writ large. They are a kind of moral instruction. They remind of something we've heard many times before but is worth repeating on a wartime Memorial Day when we're uncertain about what we celebrate. We're the land of the free for one reason only: We're also the home of the brave.

Thorsness's memoir proves this point several times over. It is a book that can provide comfort and assistance to us in our own hard times. It is also a book that can point the way to a life well lived. In its own modest style, this is a great book by a great man.

—Scott W. Johnson
November 2010

CHAPTER 1

MEDAL OF HONOR MISSION

On April 19, 1967, my backseater, Harry Johnson, and I took off from the Takhli Air Base in Thailand and headed for North Vietnam. We were counting down the few missions we had to go before reaching the magic number of 100, which provided a ticket home from Vietnam. We had about a dozen to go. By this time, we were the lead F-105F "Wild Weasel" crew.

The two-man Weasels were designed to deal with the Soviet surface-to-air missile (SAM) installations. Originally, the plane was called the Mad Mongoose, but the Air Force discovered that this name was already taken and so it became the Wild Weasel. We affectionately referred to the F-105 as the "Thud" because it was unwieldy and lumbering, but reliable with a strong heart. The guys in the bombers were particular fans because we took out the SAM sites so they made it out alive after dropping their loads.

Just a few weeks earlier, a Weasel flight usually involved a two-man crew, like Harry—the Electronic Warfare Officer (EWO)—and me, in an F-105F, and three wingmen in the single-seater F-105D. But more F-105Fs were arriving and, on the way back home after a successful mission, Harry and I came up with the idea of having two Weasels in our flight and splitting the four planes into two elements just before entering the target area. If we put one two-man Weasel along with a single seat F-105D on each side of the target, we could attack two SAM sites simultaneously instead of just one. By this point in the war, the entire North Vietnamese defense system—flak gunners, MiG pilots, SAM site operators— had set reactions when an attack—24 American planes—headed their way. Under the new scenario Harry and I worked out, by the time the Weasel flight split, they would have their game plan set and would not be able to make last-minute adjustments.

Of course, there was a down side to the plan. Splitting the flight meant that each half would have only one leader and one wingman to watch for surprise SAM launches and sneaky MiGs. And we would have less firepower. We would have just two planes with bombs to wipe out the SAMs, destroy their radar and control van, and kill the launch crew.

On April 19, our target was the Xuan Mai army barracks and a storage supply in the flat delta area 30 miles southwest of Hanoi. As we refueled over Laos, we had a flight of four F-4 Phantoms to defend us against MiGs and four flights of four F-105D strike aircraft—Thuds heavily loaded with bombs to hit the SAM installations.

The second Weasel crew in my flight was Jerry Hoblit and his EWO, Tom Wilson: both experts at their job. Jerry and I had known one another for years and had the "split-the-Weasel-flight" system down pretty good.

We were still about 80 miles from the target area when Harry radioed me, "It's going to be a busy day, we've already got two SAMs looking at us with acquisition radar, and there are bound to be more."

The closer we got, the more SAM sites were tracking us. A SAM's practical range was about 17 miles. We carried an AGM-45 SHRIKE missile that homed in on the SAM's radar, but its range was about seven miles. They got to shoot first. That was their advantage. Ours was that if they missed, we had a window of opportunity to kill them. The camouflage on their sites was useless once they launched, as the SAM kicked up debris and often left a smoke or vapor trail that we could home right onto.

As we approached our preplanned split, about 25 miles southwest of the target, our SAM scope was overflowing; no less than four sites were tracking us, plus several 85mm flak radars. To keep from alerting the enemy on the radio, we used visual signals. I gave a large fast rock of our wings, and Jerry and Tom split off.

In our pre-flight briefing, we had decided that Jerry and his wingman would take the north side of the target area, Harry and I the south.

Airborne electronic intelligence aircraft, B-66s mostly, circled at a relatively safe distance and alerted us when MiGs were airborne. They transmitted on Guard frequency—the emergency channel. When our channel and Guard transmitted at the same time, both became garbled and hard to understand. That garble added to the age-old axiom: "more combat, more confusion."

The high-pitched radio chatter was non-stop: multiple calls from the strike pilots calling out flak, MiG alerts coming over Guard channel, me listening to Harry, and Harry listening to me.

Suddenly Jerry and his wingman—Kingfish 3 and 4—were attacked by MiGs. The F-105 Weasel was never intended to be a dogfighter; it was designed to deliver nuclear weapons in a high-speed, low-altitude maneuver. Thud drivers called it a "great big airplane with itty-bitty wings." The aerodynamically superior MiG —an aircraft built for air-to-air combat—could out-turn us, but we were faster and could outrun them.

When Kingfish 3 and 4 were attacked, Jerry in Kingfish 3 called out: "Kingfish 4, burner." Jerry knew they could outrun and then outmaneuver the MiGs in afterburner. But Kingfish 4's afterburner failed. His Thud couldn't outrun the MiGs without his burner— his speed advantage was gone. Jerry, however, using all his skill-and-cunning, was able to evade the MiGs and got himself and the crippled Kingfish 4 out of the area.

By now, Harry and I and Kingfish 2 were just rolling in to bomb our second hot SAM site. "Kingfish lead," came the call from my wingman, "Kingfish 2 is hit!" As we pulled up out of our bomb run, I radioed him, "Kingfish 2, head southeast toward the hills, plug in burner, keep transmitting, and I'll home in on you." Pilot Tom Madison and EWO Tom Sterling kept transmitting. Madison soon said, "I've got more warning cockpit lights." His voice echoed the tension; things were going from bad to worse fast.

As my automatic direction finder homed in on Tom's transmission, it put them at my eleven o'clock position. As we reached the foothills I heard him again: "It is getting worse!" Within a few seconds, I heard the sickening sound of the beeper. Each parachute is equipped with a small radio transmitter attached to the lanyard of the chute. When a pilot ejects and his chute opens, the radio is activated. Each time I heard a beeper in North Vietnam, it knotted my stomach: Another American aviator had been shot down. The only good thing about hearing a beeper was that the aviator's chute opened successfully. He had a chance. Within a few seconds we heard a second beeper—both flyers were out of the aircraft and had good chutes.

I saw them floating down about two miles ahead of us, their white chutes standing out clearly against the green foothills below. Off to my left, at about 10:30, I saw movement. It was a MiG-17. There was no doubt that he was beginning a strafing run on one of the parachutes. "Harry, keep your eyes peeled, I'm setting up on the MiG!" I cranked to the left, pulled up and rolled back right, ending up a bit higher than the MiG and in a nose-down, right-bank pursuit curve. The enemy pilot was concentrating on killing our pilots in their chutes and did not see us.

At 500 mph, I quickly overtook the MiG. I squeezed the trigger of the Gatling gun, but the one-second "buzz saw" burst missed. My nose-down path took me just below the MiG and slightly to his left, about 700 feet behind him. I pulled the trigger again. This time I saw his wing come apart.

As the MiG spiraled downward and crashed, Harry called, "Leo, we got MiGs on our ass!" I snapped my head left and saw the belly of a MiG about 1,000 feet back—a bad sight. If he was a good pilot, we were dead. I snapped to the right, dumped the nose and plugged in the afterburner. For a few seconds we were in the MiG's range, but its bullets missed. In a few more seconds we were supersonic, and the MiGs quickly gave up the chase.

Our SHRIKE missile and bombs were used, and our 20mm ammo and fuel were both low. We were over the mountains west of Hanoi, out of SAM range and where MiGs were not a threat. We climbed southwest toward northern Laos and a refueling tanker.

"Brigham Control, this is Kingfish lead," I radioed to the airborne command post orbiting over southern Laos out of harm's way. "Kingfish 2, an F-105F with two crew, is down at 20'52" north latitude and 105'24" east longitude."

"Roger Kingfish lead, copy: Kingfish 2 is down. Did you see parachutes?"

"Affirmative, and two good beepers." I responded. "Advise any rescue aircraft there are a bunch of MiGs around, and the location is in SAM range."

Brigham called up the rescue aircraft—World War II-era A-1E Skyraiders, nicknamed Sandys—and a rescue helicopter. The Sandy was a great rescue plane because it could absorb heavy ground fire and fly a long way at low altitude. The Sandys' job was to make contact with the downed aviators, keep the enemy troops at bay, and direct the helicopter in if the aviators were alive and evading.

We were going out for fuel at the tanker as the Sandys were coming in. I gave them a call: "Sandy, be on your toes as you near the bailout area, there are MiGs in the area, and it is in SAM range." This rescue effort was closer to Hanoi than any other they had yet attempted; they had never even encountered MiGs or seen a SAM. Over the radio I gave the Sandys a fast "SAM evasion" briefing.

As the tanker pumped us full, we talked to Brigham, stressing again that we had to have a flight go back in with us. But the 16 Thuds, the four flights of four that had bombed Xuan Mai complex, were finished refueling and heading home to Takhli.

As we broke off from the tanker, Harry and I had a very serious, very short conversation over the intercom. "Harry, if we go back, we go it alone," I said. He was thinking the same thing that I was: Bad odds. But our two buddies were on the ground. The longer we waited before giving them cover, the greater the odds they would be captured or killed. Harry didn't object when I turned back toward North Vietnam.

As we headed in, the knot in my stomach tightened. I had promised myself never to lose a wingman in combat. I had failed. Had I made a mistake? Should I have attacked the second SAM site differently? A dozen questions posed themselves: none of them with answers.

As we approached the bailout site, Harry's voice came over the intercom: "SAM acquisition radar has us, Leo—still safe range." On Guard channel, I was periodically calling, "Kingfish 2, lead here, do you read?" Again, "Kingfish 2, lead here, please come up." After the third call, we picked up a weak transmission. There was a voice but so garbled with static that I couldn't tell if it was speaking English or Vietnamese. I knew to be careful: the Vietnamese had learned how to use our survival kit emergency radios and occasionally they tried to talk us into an area where MiGs were waiting for us.

We came over the site heading northeast just above a wafer thin cloud layer at about 18,000 feet. Looking straight down I could see the green mountains. "Leo, MiG eight o'clock!" Harry shouted. I saw another MiG at eleven o'clock. We had flown right into a "wagon wheel"—four or five MiGs in a large circle orbiting the downed pilots. Following the circle of MiGs clockwise, I picked one up and squeezed off the last burst of my Gatling gun. Pieces of the plane came off. My gun film was used up but later we were credited with a probable kill.

For the second time we had to plug in the burner, roll inverted, point 45 degrees down, and outrun the MiGs. Once we were clear, we turned north, flying just above the mountains, and headed back west toward our two downed pilots. I passed on information about the one garbled Guard transmission to the Sandys and warned them again about MiGs.

Near the shoot-down site, I started calling for Kingfish 2 again. There was no response, but then a frightened high-pitched call broke the radio silence. "Sandy 1 is going in, Sandy 1 is going in— MiGs got 'em."

"Get on the treetops," I radioed Sandy 2, "get as low, slow as you can, turn as hard as you can, and the MiGs can't get you." The Sandy was a propeller fighter with a top speed of maybe 350 knots; it can fly slower, lower, and turn tighter—that was its only advantage over the MiG. The Sandy's pilot responded, "Copy, I'll try."

Trying to sound confident, I added, "and keep talking, keep your mike button down, and we'll home in on you." He said, "Okay, but hurry, there's at least four of 'em." I dropped our nose toward the trees, grabbed about 600 mph, and wondered what I'd do when we got there.

We quickly picked up three of the MiGs. I turned hard into one of them at one o'clock. I was out of ammo—but he didn't know it. A couple of thousand feet out, I suddenly cranked hard back to the left toward a second MiG. When I was sure he saw us, I hauled back on the stick and pulled the nose up sharply and rolled inverted. My hope was that they'd think I was armed but confused and didn't know which of them to engage. If they believed that, maybe they'd let go of the Sandy, at least temporarily, and concentrate on killing us.

It worked. They all tried to get a bead on us, and the Sandy was able to scoot out through a valley at treetop level. Soon he was out of sight and safe.

By this time, Harry and I were once again in burner, twisting and turning through the mountains skimming the trees.

By now, fuel was critical. We kept calling the tanker for a rendezvous and resumed calling on Guard channel hoping, one last time, to raise one of the two Toms on their emergency radio. No response. The second Sandy had turned around and the helicopter had been canceled; the rescue attempt had failed. I had lost my wingmen. I wondered what I would write to their wives.

We switched to "tanker frequency" for a rendezvous over Laos. We were talking to the tanker when we suddenly heard: "Leo, Panda 4 here, I got 600 pounds, am lost, can you help!" It was a shock: In combat, you never use personal names. We didn't know that Brigham Control had finally found an F-105:D strike flight to help in the rescue effort—Panda flight had engaged the MiGs and shot down two of them. During the dogfight, one plane, Panda 4, became separated and then lost.

"Tanker 1, you have six minutes to rendezvous with Panda 4, or he ejects," I radioed on the Guard channel. "You gotta come farther north."

Tanker 1 responded, "Roger, Kingfish, we'll do our best." The tanker added, "and Panda 4, we are transmitting—home in on us."

During these brief calls with Panda 4 and the tanker, Harry and I discussed our fuel state. Our plane and Panda 4 were far apart: the tanker could only get to one of us. Even if we didn't get fuel, Harry and I agreed that we had a chance at making it to the Mekong River—the divide between Laos and Thailand—before flaming out. If we got past the Mekong, we could eject over friendly territory. But if Panda 4 didn't refuel, he would have to eject over enemy territory. It was an easy choice: the tanker belonged to Panda.

Heading south, we climbed to 35,000 feet to suck the most miles from our nearly empty tanks. Harry dialed in Udorn Air Base, 30 miles south of the Mekong in Thailand. We were 130 miles from the runway. The F-105 can glide two miles for each 1,000 feet lost. If we kept the engine running until we hit 100 miles, we could glide to friendly territory even if we had to eject before reaching the Udorn runway.

I called Udorn tower and explained that if we made it there, we would need a straight-in approach. Then Harry and I silently stared at our fuel gauge as it dropped toward zero. At 70 miles to the Mekong I pulled the throttle to idle and slowed to the plane's best glide speed: 270 knots (310 mph). In 15 minutes, we would travel 70 miles and glide across the river into Thailand.

Luck was on our side. With fuel indicating empty, the engine ran until we made it to Udorn, turned straight in on the southeast-headed runway and landed. Just after we touched down the engine shut off.

Harry matter-of-factly said, "That was a full day's work."

It was true. We had delivered our payload, shot down two enemy fighters in a plane not designed for aerial combat, kept our wingmen from getting murdered in their parachutes, and saved another U.S. aircraft. But as I retracted the canopy and stepped out of the plane, I felt like a failure, dejected at having left two good men behind in the jungles of North Vietnam where they had probably been captured—or even worse—by now. If someone had told me then that I would receive the Medal of Honor for this mission, I would not have believed him. If he had told me that I'd learn about receiving the Medal of Honor while I was in a Hanoi prison, I still would not have believed him.

CHAPTER 2

SHOT DOWN

On the morning of April 30, a little less than two weeks after this mission, I was awakened by the alarm at 4:30 a.m. My routine each morning I flew a mission was the same: up too early, shower, don boots and flying suit, breakfast at the O club, and bike it to the field. When I got there, the weather and intelligence guys were scurrying around preparing for the briefing. Pilots were getting coffee as they checked today's primary and backup targets. Some mornings were happy: an easy mission in western or southern North Vietnam. Some mornings were somber: another effort to try and knock down the Doumer Bridge on Hanoi's north side. Every time that bridge was targeted we lost at least one plane.

This morning's mission was successful. The strike force destroyed most of the supply depot that was its chief target. Our Weasels killed the threatening SAM site, and all 24 of our airplanes made it home. Harry and I smiled at each other as we got out of the cockpit, knowing that we had ticked off another mission, and now had only eight left before we reached the magic number and headed home.

A rule in the 355 Tactical Fighter Wing was that if you flew the morning mission, you didn't fly the afternoon mission. It's a full day's job being strapped in the cockpit under high pressure for four or five hours. And the Weasel missions were always the longest—first in and last out—which meant that we were regularly in the extreme threat area for 12 to 15 minutes.

Each strike force usually had at least two spares. If a pilot had to abort because of maintenance problems, one of the spares, waiting in an aircraft, immediately started his engine, and filled in. On this afternoon, we were the only Weasel crew available as a spare. The odds are that spares don't go, but as we waited in the plane, one of the Weasels scheduled to go had a maintenance abort, so off we went on our second mission of the day. It was not a particularly hard one; the target was 50 miles west of Hanoi, and when we completed it we would only have seven missions to go.

As soon as we were airborne, little things started going wrong. Someone's emergency parachute beeper triggered on. We couldn't figure out whose it was so it beeped on and on. The refueling track was changed after takeoff, which added some temporary confusion. Just small things, but taken together they had the feel of premonition.

And there was another disconcerting thing that afternoon. It was not mechanical or electrical; it was the pilot. I had a knottier feel than usual in my stomach, a vague sense of not-rightness. It felt less like foreboding than forewarning. But I couldn't pin it down and said nothing to Harry.

We were scheduled to launch against a known hot SAM site. Our turn point was a large mountain peak a bit south of the Red River, about 70 miles west of Hanoi. As we came over the mountain peak, we accelerated to 600 knots. A minute before launch, we picked up a loud air-to-air warning signal. Some seven to eight miles behind the Weasel flight was the F-4 Phantom flight providing defense against MiGs. When we got the air-to-air signal, I called the leader, "Cadillac here, we've got air-to-air on us." He responded, "Roger, I have you on our radar." He left the impression that their radar was triggering our air-to-air signal.

In fact, two MiGs were orbiting in the valley just behind our mountain peak checkpoint. We had gone directly over them. At 600 knots the MiGs could not keep up with us, but they didn't have to. As we passed over them heading east, they happened to be turning east in their orbit. All they had to do was pull up and hit us with their Atoll air-to-air missiles. We took one right up the tailpipe.

The Weasel shook violently; it felt like we'd been smacked by a massive sledgehammer. The stick and rudder pedals immediately went limp; the cockpit filled with heavy black smoke.

Harry and I knew that the maximum ejection speed for an F-105 was 525 knots. But we also knew of pilots whose Thuds had exploded while taking the time to slow down. We had decided that if we were ever hit hard we would eject immediately.

I shouted "GO!" Harry knew that if he hesitated to blow his canopy and I ejected before he did, my rocket would throw fire directly into the rear cockpit. He said, "Shit!" and, as I heard his canopy blow and seat eject, I pulled my handle.

Vivid in my mind to this day is the feeling of catapulting into the slipstream doing nearly 600 knots (690 mph). My helmet ripped off, my body felt as though it had been flung against a wall, and my legs flailed outward. Two seconds later, the chute opened, violently yanking me upward. My body rotated a couple of times, then settled into a float.

Falling downward, I tried to take stock. When I cleared the cockpit, the wind had apparently caught my lower legs and forced my knees straight sideways at about 90 degrees. My boots were still on but the little pencil-sized zipper pockets on my sleeves were ripped away. As I looked up at my chute I saw that at least a quarter of the panels were ripped open; I would be slamming into the ground faster than normal—with destroyed knees.

One bright spot: a mile or two to the east I could see Harry's chute. I did not know at the time, but my wingman Bob Abbott had also been shot down by an Atoll.

The sky was full of F-105s. Colonel Jack Broughton, our wing commander and the strike force commander that day, had obviously diverted some or all of the planes to help the three of us floating down into enemy territory.

When you are doing zero airspeed dangling in a parachute, and a Thud zips by 100 feet away at 500 knots giving a thumbs up, it is a loud thrill. I pulled out my emergency radio from the pocket attached to the parachute harness. I pushed the "press to talk" button and gave them my name—then added, "Get me out of here!"

We had ejected at about 10,000 feet and so had several minutes of float time before we hit. Many thoughts I had then are still crystal clear today. I thought about my wife Gaylee and our daughter

Dawn, who were at Nellis Air Force Base in Nevada. Gaylee and I had many fighter-pilot friends at Nellis. Some had come to Takhli before I did and some of those had been shot down and captured, or, worse yet, never heard from or about again. I felt devastated for what my wife and daughter might be forced to endure. My floating-down thought was: "If I'm killed when I hit the ground, will they ever find out?" I felt guilty, too: reasoning that I had failed them. I was putting them in what could be years of limbo.

With the ground getting larger and larger below me, I also felt that I must have made a mistake and that what was about to happen to Harry and me was my fault. I knew the odds were high that I would be killed or captured within the hour, especially because my knees would not support an attempt at evasion. But there was another thought that alternated with the guilt that flooded me—a voice, actually, rather than a thought. It was loud and clear and kept repeating like a tape loop, "Leo, you are going to make it.... Leo, you are going to make it...." It was the first time in my life that the Lord preemptively answered my prayers. The voice and these words would stay with me for the next six years. This was God's gift to me as I descended into a nightmare.

I was still 2,000 to 3,000 feet in the air when something in a small darker area in the jungle caught my eye. I concentrated and realized that it was muzzle flashes. They were shooting at me!

As I entered the canopy of jungle, I remembered to cross my legs. Branches banged and slapped as I readied to hit hard on bad knees. Suddenly I stopped, bounced a bit and hung still. I looked up and saw that my chute had caught on a dead branch. I was maybe 40 feet off the ground. Just to my right was a tall stand of bamboo. I swung to reach for a stalk, thinking to grab hold, undo my chute releases and shinny down to the ground. But I couldn't get a good grip on the bamboo. We carried a one-inch-wide nylon lanyard in our g-suit for just this situation. I finally got it out, tied it above the quick releases, tried to wrap it around my waist and leg and let loose the releases. I used ten valuable minutes getting to the ground.

I was part way up the side of a mountain. My knees buckled each time I tried to stand. Thuds continued to fly over my downed position but I doubted they could see me through the trees. I tried one more call on my emergency radio—both my transmission and theirs were so garbled I could not make out words.

I heard voices below me. I crawled on all fours up the hill.

The going was slow; they were gaining on me. A Thud flew over and the bad guys took cover. I crawled faster, hoping to find a clearing before they found me. If they had an opening, the Thuds could strafe the jungle around me, hold the bad guys back and maybe, just maybe, a chopper would show up to pluck me out.

But there was no opening and no helicopter. Knowing I was theirs, the North Vietnamese hollered excitedly when they drew near. I rolled on my back to face them. There were a dozen or more: all young males, maybe 15–20 years old. Most were armed with machetes. I saw one real rifle, an old one, and a couple of wooden rifles, probably for training.

They grabbed my feet and arms, and sat me upright. One pulled out a black cloth bag—pillow-case size. The last thing I saw just before he slipped it over my head was the hate-filled eyes of a young Vietnamese pulling back a machete to strike me. Perhaps it was fatigue or excess adrenalin, but I had no fear.

The machete blow never came. Instead there were a couple of minutes of excited jabber and then the bag came off. They stood me on my feet; my knees collapsed. They stood me on my feet again; my knees collapsed again. The third time they held me upright and began cutting off my clothes: g-suit; boots, flying suit, t-shirt; everything but my bloody shorts.

They insisted that I walk, but I couldn't. They decided to make me walk by beating me. Eventually my collapsing knees convinced them that I wasn't pretending. With sign language, I tried to explain that I wanted a machete to split bamboo, tie a strip on the inside and outside of my legs above and below my knees. They split the bamboo. Eventually four took belts from their pants and I used them to tie the bamboo to my legs. Of course the strips cut into my knees and legs, and stayed in place just a few steps. After a couple of tries, my body and mind gave out. I collapsed into unconsciousness.

I came to in the center of a large net. They had cut two poles, crossed and tied them in the middle, attached the net corners on each pole beyond the cross. Four men hustled me down the mountain.

Well past dark, we came to a large hut, perhaps 20 by 40 feet, on stilts, surrounded by a group of women and children. They carried me inside. The floor was made of large bamboo poles. The walls appeared to be woven mats. Dried bamboo torches lighted the darkness. Men were squatting along the walls smoking opium pipes. Harry was already there, also in dirty bloody underwear, spread-eagled on his back with wrists and ankles tied. Soon I was in the same position next to him.

Harry and I spoke now and then, although when we did they hit us. Neither of us understood a word of Vietnamese. We both had heard stories that captured American flyers were summarily executed. The conversation around us finally slackened; an older man stood, looked down at us and spoke to the others. Obviously a decision had been made. Knowing the words would cause me a beating, I had to say, "Harry, I think this is a trial, and we may be executed tonight." In that frightful setting, I will never forget, nor fail to appreciate, Harry's comforting response. "Leo, either they will or won't, we can't control it. No sense worrying about it."

It was the beginning of an ordeal that would brutalize me, and, paradoxically for anyone who didn't share the unique experience of the POWs, also allow me to become a better and fuller person.

CHAPTER 3

WHAT I BROUGHT WITH ME

As I lay there I wondered whether, if the North Vietnamese allowed me to live, I could survive—not just physically, but mentally and morally. Would I break? And if I did, would the failure stay with me forever? These were some of the questions that swarmed into my head in that hut in the mountains of North Vietnam. Most of all I wondered if my 35 years of freedom had prepared me for what lay ahead.

Born into the Depression in 1932, I was a Minnesota farm kid from what always seemed to me a typical family. Mother and father, older sister and brother. My parents didn't get past the eighth grade; their education came from working the land on a farm near the town of Walnut Grove where they settled after getting married.

My dad was not much of a talker, but he was a good worker and I learned from that. He believed in the American Dream and was ambitious. Even as a young farmer with his own fields to till, he hired himself out to work for others, digging potatoes and picking corn by hand. When my brother John and I were old enough, dad bought a hay baler and converted a 1932 Chevy coupe into a tractor to pull it. We baled alfalfa for other farmers; it was hard and itchy work.

Later on I would discover that we had been poor—working hard to scratch out an existence. But we never went hungry, and we never had to sell our land. If we were poor economically, we were rich in love and responsibility. Like most of our neighbors we felt lucky to be who we were and had no doubts about America, for the present or the future.

Farmers raise food. So we fed ourselves. It wasn't always sweet corn necessarily, but new field corn tastes almost as good. Our oats went into our cattle, hogs, and chickens. We sold our barley and wheat and made our own flour. Cattle supplied a lot of our needs. A horse-drawn manure spreader fertilized the fields. Using a hand-operated milk separator, we were able to sell the cream and to make cottage cheese. The family drank the skim milk, and the rest put weight on the hogs. When the cows passed calving age, we had them for dinner. Chickens gave eggs to eat and to sell for grocery money; when the hens and roosters passed their prime, they, too, went into the pot. We hand-pumped water from the well and had a cistern in the basement. In summer, a nearby lake offered an easy way to clean off the day's grime from shucking grain and slopping the hogs. In the winter, coal and corn cobs heated the water in which we bathed and washed our clothes.

We defeated the Depression one day at a time. Spread-eagled on that rough bamboo floor, I told myself that I would have to fight captivity the same way.

——————

Samuel Johnson once said that the prospect of death concentrates the mind wonderfully. This was certainly true in my case. Like most people, I had skated along the surface of life assuming that things would always be good and taking for granted the miraculous gifts I had been granted. There was no question in that hut about what truly mattered to me: family, faith, and friends. Family was constantly—almost obsessively—on my mind in those first hours: my parents, sister and brother, but most of all my wife and daughter. I realized sadly that they too were about to become prisoners, trapped by my captivity.

I was physically bound—bound into my pain, so to speak. My mind was my only escape. I built a memory room in those first hours of imprisonment. It wasn't fancy. It was a lot like the tree house I built in our farm grove as a seventh grader. I used the old lumber piled behind our barn, adding a crude door and tin sheets from a torn-down hen house for the roof. I sawed a few boards and two-by-fours and nailed in a couple of crude shelves. It was a perfectly serviceable memory room.

I used the old egg crates we kept in the barn to store my memories. Three crates were labeled Family, Faith, and Fun. Soon I added another, for Friends. So much of my life involved airplanes that I added a fifth crate: Flying. Underlying every memory was the worry about what my wife and daughter were thinking. Had they heard yet? Are they busy constructing memory houses too?

The image of Gaylee shimmered in my mind. I met her after graduating from Walnut Grove High School in the fall of 1950. Knowing I would have to put myself through college, I had enrolled at neighboring South Dakota State in Brookings. Right away I learned that my high school strengths—sports, girls, and hunting—wouldn't help me academically. After finishing a quarter at Brookings, I made a wise decision: Join the military, grow up, decide what I wanted to do in life, and perhaps use the GI bill later on to help pay for college after I got some real-life experience.

We Midwesterners thought of the military first when we were arranging our lives. My older cousin was killed in World War II, my future brothers-in-law all served in the war—one was killed in a B-17—and my brother was serving with distinction in Korea when I was serving without distinction in college. So in December 1950, I signed up for a four-year enlisted hitch in the U.S. Air Force.

While I left South Dakota State with no degree or academic achievement, I didn't come away empty-handed. I had made an excellent decision the first day during registration. The lines were alphabetical: A-F, G-L, M-R, and S-Z. I was a "T" and therefore in the fourth line. But I noticed the cutest girl there, Gaylee Anderson, was in the first line. I was smart enough to step to the end of the first line and stand behind her. By the time Gaylee finished registering, I had reserved a dance with her at the freshman ball that evening.

I was immediately addicted to her effervescence and sense of humor. There was much in common between us: She was from South Dakota, of Swedish stock, and I was from Minnesota, of Norwegian stock. The "Scandinavian thing" would always be a subject of banter. Shortly after I got home from my six years of imprisonment in Hanoi, we were at dinner with two couples from our church. As usual, there were many questions about the POW experience. In response to a question from one of our dinner partners, I said, "Without question, those were the most significant six years of my life." He immediately looked at Gaylee and said mischievously, "What do you think about that? You were not with him during his most significant six years?" Gaylee thought a moment, and then responded, "Well, if Leo says those were the most significant years of his life, he means it." Then she added, "Of course, he's Norwegian. If he'd been a Swede, he could have done it in three."

After three months of dating and three years of letters from Air Force bases, we were married during Christmas leave in 1953. A year later we had a beautiful, healthy daughter who was 11 years old when I left for Vietnam in 1966.

I wanted to savor memories of Gaylee, so instead of using them all up quickly in the mountain hut, I moved for a while to the box that held recollections of flying, the other passion of my life.

It had taken me a while to become a flyer—two years as an enlisted man before the Aviation Cadet Program opened up because the Air Force needed pilots for Korea. I applied and was accepted and briefly entered a limbo where I was looked at with disdain by enlisted personnel who thought I was putting on airs by trying to become an officer—and by officers who thought the same thing.

By January 1953, I was at Lackland Air Force Base in San Antonio, Texas, beginning 15 months of training on how to be a pilot and officer. The three basic parts of the program were military training, academics, and flying. The military training came easy: I already knew how to march, stand at attention, and pass inspection. Then came three months of books. Finally we got to the fun part: flying. As a kid I was a good athlete. Throwing, batting, kicking, running all came easily. I felt that flying would be the same. But there was one problem: I am left-handed.

My flight instructor at Goodfellow Air Force Base in San Angelo, Texas, was Lieutenant Luellan. Our training aircraft progressed from basic to advanced: L-21 to T-6 to T-28 to T-33. The

L-21 was a little two-seat tandem Piper Cub. It was a tail dragger: the main gear under the wings and the third wheel under the tail. (L-21 was its military name; all civilian aviators know it as the "Super Cub.") Its 125-horsepower engine hurled you along at least 100 mph.

When the day for my first flight finally came, Lieutenant Luellan told me to grab my parachute and follow him. We walked across the ramp to the flying machine, where he said, "Follow me and watch what I check on the walk around." After some explanation of what was important besides the fuel and oil levels, he said, "Okay Thorsness, you fly from the front seat—try it on."

With eagerness and a bit of apprehension I climbed in, cramming my own bulk and that of my parachute into the tiny cockpit. The lieutenant continued, "Get your feet down there on the rudders, lock your shoulder harness into your seat belt and snug them both down." His next instruction was, "In the middle there, sticking up between your legs, is the control stick." I confidently grabbed the control stick—with my left hand, of course. I quickly scanned the few instruments on the control panel and glanced back over my right shoulder where Lieutenant Luellan was watching. With obvious disbelief, he said, "The throttle is over there on the left side panel." I looked at my grip on the control stick, looked over to the left side and saw the little lever with a knob on top. It was obvious that the throttle was important and would have to be continuously held while flying. So I did what was logical: reached with my right hand across my left hand and forearm that was holding the control stick and gripped the throttle. I instantly knew that this was not a good way to impress a flight instructor. The lieutenant simply shook his head as he walked away after staring for a moment at my crossed arms.

In the memory box I searched while being held captive in the mountains of North Vietnam, I found something I'd almost forgotten about: a near fatal mistake when I had progressed to the more advanced T-6 "Texan" trainer. It also happened at Goodfellow. I was flying solo and entered the downwind leg—parallel to the runway about a mile away, heading due south at 1,000 feet above the ground and at about 100 knots (115 mph). When I was about half a mile past the end of the runway, I made a 90-degree turn to the east. I felt I was doing well—beginning to lose an appropriate amount of altitude and slow the aircraft.

A good checkpoint, in addition to the runway, was the Goodfellow football field near the end of the runway, and just slightly to the east. I didn't realize until I was nearly through my 90-degree turn onto final approach that the wind was blowing me a good bit off course. Panicking, I realized I would overshoot and be more lined up with the football field than the runway.

Two of the best bits of aviation advice I remember receiving in flying school came from a crusty old aviator, Captain Malone ("crusty old" at that stage of my life meant that he was 27), who told me, "There are old pilots and bold pilots, but no old bold pilots." He added, "Never exceed your limits, or the airplane's limits, and you will live to be an old man." As I approached Goodfellow—low to the ground, without extra airspeed, and overshooting the final approach—I was contradicting all his maxims at once.

I turned too sharply, dipping my left wing down too far. I was losing lift. To counter, I stupidly applied a bit of right aileron. Bingo! I'd just set up a snap roll.

If I had done the logical thing—reversing and trying to roll back to the right—it would have been over. It was much faster and used less altitude to accelerate the roll all the way around and back to level wings. Call it instinct, luck, divine intervention, whatever—it was a lesson that vividly lived in my memory room's Flying box.

As I thought about it, I realized that the process that had made me a flyer had also made me a man. I had entered the Air Force because I didn't have anything else to do. But I soon discovered that I had found a profession rather than just a place to bide time. Once I was married and a father, I wanted to get ahead, and the Air Force let me. I attended night classes offered by the University of Maryland while we were stationed from 1959 to 1963 at Spangdahlem Air Base in Germany. (That was the height of the Cold War and, in four years in Germany, I rotated regular work, night classes, and 72-hour tours sitting at the end of the runway with a nuclear bomb in an F-105 bomb bay. We slept in concrete bunkers near the end of the runway so we could be airborne within 15 minutes if the "bell went off.") After four years of study and night school, I was within six months of receiving my degree. When we left Germany for Nellis Air Force Base in Las Vegas, I was allowed to stop at the University of Omaha and finish.

At Nellis, I continued night school aiming for a master's degree in aerospace operations management from the University of Southern California. (We rented a house in Los Angeles so that both Dawn and I could register for school, and I returned to Nellis every month to fly enough hours to stay current in the F-105.) Each quarter I had one engineering course and two or three other courses. The other courses I aced. But engineering was a nightmare. (Literally: when I was in the Hanoi Hilton, I had recurring dreams of trying to cope with these courses and would wake up momentarily thankful that I was in North Vietnam rather than at USC.) Gaylee, who was good at math, helped me, but most nights I stayed up until 2 or 3 a.m. memorizing formulas I didn't understand and math concepts I had never heard of.

After miraculously receiving the degree, I cleaned out our West Covina rental home, and returned to Nellis. The first day at work the operations officer said, "Welcome back, Leo. Congratulations. And, by the way, this morning your assignment to Southeast Asia came in. You were at the top of the heap—lots of F-105 flying time and good gunnery and bombing scores. You are now a Wild Weasel."

CHAPTER 4

DOWN THE MOUNTAIN

After a hard, sleepless night in the bamboo hut, Harry and I were untied and moved a few miles to the edge of the foothills. We arrived just as light was breaking and were locked in adjacent rooms in a small building. A wooden cot was the only furniture. I was asleep within minutes. But I awoke almost immediately to the sound of loud noises in the next room. It was Harry being taken out. "I'm hurt," I heard him shout in response to whatever orders the North Vietnamese were giving him.

Fifteen minutes later I heard him stumble back into his room. Then there was a jingling of keys—a sound that would soon take on sinister implications—and my door opened. They let me use sticks for support as I dragged myself out. As I passed Harry's door, he hollered, "Geneva Convention, Leo. Hold out." I shouted back: "Do my best."

We had all been taught about the Geneva Convention when we entered the military. And before going into combat, we were briefed in more detail, particularly about Article 2, which states that when captured, a prisoner of war is obligated only to give four pieces of information: name, rank, serial number, and date of birth. Captors are not supposed to ask for more and are specifically barred from using physical or mental means to obtain it.

These four items formed a mantra I repeated to myself as I was escorted outside. I recognized the smell of hogs, a strong farm memory. The North Vietnamese motioned me around the corner and sure enough, there were several scrawny pigs in a pen. A guard opened the gate and moved me forward. Then came a push from behind and I was face down in the muck. I rolled onto my back and looked up. In barely understandable English, a guard said, "Name?" With as much dignity as someone in bloody shorts lying in pig shit could muster, I said, "Thorsness, Leo K; Major; AO3025937; February 14, 1932."

Next he said, "What target?"

I replied: "Thorsness, Leo K; Major, AO3025937; February 14, 1932."

"Bad answer," he snarled and threatened me with a thick stick. "Tomorrow target?" he tried again.

I got as far as, "Thorsness, Leo," when the stick smacked me.

I stayed with name, rank, serial number, and date of birth as an answer to each question. The guard stayed with the stick. It hurt badly, but I could stand it. As they dragged me back I said, "Okay," when I passed Harry's door. "Good," he answered.

I got a plate of dirty steamed rice and not enough water. My body and mind were totally spent, and I fell in and out of fitful sleep for the next few hours, waking several times to the sounds of trucks. I knew that their trucks traveled mostly at night; they were a great target of opportunity during the day on our missions over North Vietnam.

I woke for good when I heard the keys jingling again. The door opened, and they motioned me to walk down the corridor. I could hear mob sounds. With my walking sticks in hand, I moved slowly out the door and in the direction of a military truck. It was perhaps 100 yards away. North Vietnamese peasants lined both sides of a worn path. As I started down the gauntlet, they crowded toward me, becoming a sea of fists and angry faces.

The guards acted as cheerleaders, riling the crowd even more. The peasants spit at me and hit me; threw stones, dirt clumps, and fists. They knocked away my walking sticks. I got up and was knocked down again. Then I was on all fours crawling as well as I could. Finally the guards began to yell at the peasants, shoving them back and dragging me toward the truck. Grabbing the tailgate, I pulled myself upright. The guards pushed me onto the truck bed, then two of them jumped in and forced me onto my back. As I stretched my arms I touched the truck-bed edge on the left, and a body on the right. "Is that you, Harry?" I asked. "It's me, Leo," he replied. A guard shouted, "NO TALK," and hit us both.

In a few minutes we were on a bumpy road with the angry mob receding behind us. The roads were bad, and we were often bounced off the truck-bed floor. If I tried to roll on my side or put my hand behind my head as a cushion, the guard kicked me.

After three or four hours, I could see a few lights and buildings out of the back of the truck. We were on a paved road now, making several turns. The truck stopped and backed up to a large gate. We were there: the infamous Hoa Lo prison in Hanoi—the Hanoi Hilton. Harry and I were dragged out of the back of the vehicle and separated. It would be three years before I got a glimpse of Harry again across the prison yard—the guard opened my cell door a couple of seconds before Harry was back inside his cell. It was three more years before I talked to Harry as we were loaded onto the bus heading for Gia Lam airport and our flight to freedom.

———

My interrogation started immediately. The setting was ominous. The walls in the small room where they put me were knobby with hand-daubed concrete. (It hurts a lot more when you are knocked against knobs than against smooth walls). The interrogators sat in two wooden chairs behind a narrow plain table; they could look down intimidatingly at me when I was allowed to sit on a short wooden stool in front of them. There was a sinister pile of paraphernalia in the corner of the room: ropes, nylon straps, two metal u-bolts with a one-inch eye on each end of the bolt, and a long metal rod.

The questions came at me like anti-aircraft flak. What was your target? What is the target tomorrow? What is your squadron? Who is your squadron commander? What is your wife's name? I gave the Geneva Convention answer. That didn't work. One of the guards hit me in the head and knocked me off the stool. Then they forced me to lean into the knobby wall with feet far back and my face touching it as they hit me from behind. They grabbed my hair and yanked me around the room, then slammed me to the floor. After they put me in a sitting position, they fastened bars to my ankles through the eyes of the u-bolts; they tied the nylon-strap ends to my upper arms over my back. As they twisted the strap tighter and tighter, I felt as though I was being separated into pieces.

Elbows are not designed to touch behind your back, but this can happen if your shoulders are popped out of their joints. When the white-hot pain failed to produce correct answers, they pressed my elbows together behind my back and doubled me forward, forcing my head down toward my legs. Later I learned that the POWs called this the "suitcase trick" because they are trying to fold you up. It was pain beyond painful.

What did they want? The equipment we flew in combat and our weapons were not new. The F-105 and F-4 Phantom were good aircraft but had been around many years. The bombs we dropped were identical to those used in World War II—"dumb bombs" that obeyed the rules of gravity. The North Vietnamese already had most of what they needed to plan their defenses against our airplanes and weapons.

But soon I understood. It was not information they wanted, but propaganda: to get American military officers to condemn the war. They pursued this objective with single-minded brutality. That was what our torture, indeed our entire imprisonment was about. They believed that POWs condemning the United States for fighting a war of aggression against "a small peaceful nation" would influence American politicians and the American public. They were right about politicians and public opinion being the key to the war's outcome; they were wrong about us being willing to do anything that would influence either.

The suitcase trick was just one torture. Another was to wrench the elbows behind the back, and tie them with a rope or wire that cut off circulation. The longer circulation was cut off to the lower arms and hands, the more painful it was when blood began to flow again: an excruciating pain. In addition to stopping blood flow, nerves were frequently damaged. After one such torture session, they ordered me, "Now write that you apologize for bombing our peace-loving Vietnamese people and demand that the American imperialist government stop bombing." The feeling in my hands was gone. Even if I had been willing to write a statement, there was no way to use a pencil, even holding one hand with the other. The North Vietnamese were not big on irony: They didn't see anything amiss with torturing someone until he agreed to write a statement saying that he was being treated humanely and leniently.

Each of us had a different threshold of pain. Each reached the breaking point at a different moment. The rule old-hands tried to pass to new prisoners as quickly as possible was this: "You cannot give information because of verbal abuse. You must take physical punishment until you are on the verge of losing your mental capacity to be rational. When you reach that point: lie, cheat, and do whatever you have to do to stay sane. Whatever lies you tell, keep them simple so you can remember them."

The prison guards and interrogators, of course, wanted to do their job—even if it was torturing someone—with the least effort. The harder they had to work to extract anything from you, the less frequently they used you. Some POWs, once broken, had so little resistance left that they were used over and over to make statements. They became the North Vietnamese's go-to guys.

Between interrogations, I was kept in the Heartbreak Hotel. This block of seven small cells—each about six by seven feet—was the most feared place in the Hanoi Hilton. On each side of the cell was a cement slab with old-fashioned stocks. The bottom half of the stocks was attached to the cement slab and had half-moon-shaped indents. I was placed on the slab face up with my ankles in the indents and the top hinged part was locked over them. The stocks were rusty and tight. Within minutes the pain started. It wasn't long until sores developed on my ankles, draining and scabbing over. When the stock was unlocked and opened; it ripped off the scabs.

For a couple of days I had no urge to urinate or have a bowel movement. I finally peed in the corner by a six-inch opening in the cell floor, which the rats used to come in and out. I was in the stock when I finally had a strong urge to defecate. I called for the guard several times. There was no response. I hurt badly and didn't want to be more miserable by lying in my own feces. The aluminum drinking cup they had given me was within reach. I was able to turn just enough and bend my knees just enough to squeeze the cup somewhat below my anus. Much of the feces went into it. I flicked it toward the corner. I had enough urine to "wash" the cup mostly free of feces. The next drink from my cup was not pleasant—but the thirst at Heartbreak was unbearable and water was so rare that you couldn't waste it.

———

I would say that my 18 days and nights of interrogations were unendurable if I hadn't endured. For much of that time I lived in a knot of pain I can only compare to that produced by a dentist's drill. I'm convinced that I survived only because of the hallucinations that became a sort of refuge for me—when I was being tortured and in between torture sessions. They were a form of mental anesthesia.

Often I felt perched on a little bench up in the corner of the cell looking down at myself—that piece of meat being worked over by the North Vietnamese. Some hallucinations were fuzzy; some vivid, such as one about a little angel. Without effort he came through the locked cell door and had a small bucket of water, which he poured into my mouth. (I recall that some spilled over my cheeks.) The problem was that no matter how many times he poured water into my mouth, it never satisfied my thirst. Finally it dawned on me: This was heavenly water, the water of life.

My father also visited me. He had died some years earlier, at the age of 57, much too young. We'd had a good relationship, but he was a quiet man who devoted all his energy to keeping our family afloat in hard times. When he was alive, we worked together and talked about the farm. But we didn't have much time for discussion of the important things. Now I could "call him up" almost anytime and spend hours talking with him. He was my companion during the darkest moments. I leaned on his strength.

I could also call up old friends, people Gaylee and I had known in our life together. Even in my hallucinations, however, there was a certain reality principle: I was always in prison, and they weren't. The friends discussed this fact and were always sympathetic, but however much they pitied me, things were good for them—their health, their marriages, their jobs—and not for me. This bothered me, and I'd summon someone else. But it was always the same story: all good for them, all bad for me.

I became so addicted to these hallucinations, and so adept at arranging them, that once when I emerged from a torture session and was briefly put in a holding cell with another POW, I offered to summon his wife and tell her he was alive. Naturally he gave me a strange look before skeptically saying, "Okay." So I closed my eyes and called her. I told her he was alive. I asked how her kids were and she said fine. I opened my eyes and told him his wife was fine, and so were his kids—the four girls. That got his attention—he indeed had four girls. But he also had three boys, a fact that never penetrated my altered state.

———

My back was broken and refrozen during these first torture sessions. My knees were further damaged. My body was wrenched apart. There was nothing particularly imaginative about the North Vietnamese techniques. They hadn't improved much on the devices of the Spanish Inquisition. They bent things that didn't bend; they separated things meant to stay together. At times I couldn't tell if I was screaming or imagining that I was screaming.

When we finally came home, several journalists, perhaps annoyed by the brief support for the war our stories of our captivity had generated, skeptically implied that when we said torture we actually meant intimidation, coercion, and degradation. But the reality of the torture we experienced was engraved on our bodies. We later calculated that some 65 POWs died from torture during the years of captivity—nearly 20 percent of all those imprisoned. Some, like Lance Sijan, were tortured so long and so hard that they simply withered away. Others, like Earl Cobeil, were tortured so expertly by some of the Cubans working for the North Vietnamese that their minds stopped working and they no longer felt pain and eventually died.

There were three Cubans, headed by a sadist we called "Fidel," at the Hanoi Hilton. They ran a little program called "Operation

Submission," focusing on eight POWs who had been more or less picked at random for extreme torture intended as on-the-job training for the North Vietnamese. (I was number eight-and-a-half and only got a sampling. I particularly remember being on the floor with Fidel working me over as he played Nancy Sinatra's "These Boots Are Made for Walking" on the phonograph.) The Cubans frequently told us, "You will do everything and anything we ask you to do before we're finished with you." Earl was their research project. They killed him from within. A POW who had been his cellmate later told me that he saw "Fidel" hit Earl directly between the eyes with a rubber hose, but Earl was so bad off that he didn't even blink. This POW had to pry Earl's teeth apart to put rice in his mouth, but eventually could not keep him alive. (While still in prison, several of us pledged $1,000 each to find someone to find and kill "Fidel"—it didn't work out.)

Our loved ones were tortured too. After he bailed out, Captain Charles Shelton was seen on the ground, destroying his radio. But he never made it to the camps and was likely killed where he landed. But the Pentagon didn't know for sure, and for 20 years kept promoting him to higher rank. This encouraged his wife to keep up hope. Eventually, after a lengthy review, Shelton was declared presumptively dead and his wife committed suicide, one of the last victims of the North Vietnamese.

――――

When I broke—when I went beyond name, rank, serial number, and date of birth—it was the lowest point in all my six years of captivity. When floating down in my parachute, I believed I had failed my family. If I died when I hit the ground, they might never know what happened to me. I also felt that I had failed my profession by allowing myself to be shot down in the first place. But these feelings were small in comparison to what I experienced when I broke under torture. I had friends who were already in the POW system. I knew they must have emerged from the same horrific torture that had broken me with their honor intact. But I had failed. Strapped on a slab, I tried to cry. But I was past tears. If I ever saw my fellow POWs, I wouldn't be able to hold my head up.

After eighteen days, they pulled me out of solitary in Heartbreak —along with a naval pilot who had been shot down two weeks after I was, Ev Southwick. They moved us to the Zoo and pushed us into a cell with Jim Hiteshew. Jim, badly injured, was lying on the center of three bed boards. We said hello and told him our names; Ev adding that he was Navy. I said that I was Air Force out of Takhli Air Base in Thailand. Jim, almost entirely covered in a cast, said, "Hi, Leo, I'm Jim Hiteshew. We knew each other at Takhli." We had both changed so much in six weeks we didn't recognize each other.

Jim was an Air Force major shot down six weeks before I was. He had ejected at the bottom of a dive run doing about 600 knots, breaking both legs and one arm so badly that the Vietnamese had almost let him die in the field. But he had refused to give up and they had reluctantly brought him in, putting him in close to a full body cast covering both legs, his chest, the lower half of his back, and one arm. They left a small opening so he could defecate and urinate. Jim needed help to survive.

Ev looked me over and said, "You're in bad shape. We've got to get you back on your feet so we can both help Jim."

I immediately began to tell them I had failed. As soon as they knew what I was talking about, Jim said roughly, "Knock it off, Leo. Don't you know?"

"Know what?"

"That everyone who goes through that type of interrogation has one of two things happen: either they broke or died—some did both."

There was—and there still is—no way for me to express my absolute euphoria at hearing these words. I was not a failure. I was average and happy to be so.

CHAPTER 5

TAP CODE

M y six years as a POW were divided into two more or less equal periods. The first three years were brutal. I lived in solitary confinement or with one or two other POWs in a small cell. If the guards heard any sound, we were instantly beaten or made to kneel for hours on rough concrete. The last three years were more of a routine. Fifteen to 45 POWs lived together in big cells. We could talk out loud.

More American aviators were shot down in 1967, the year I was shot down, than any other year of the war. So when I arrived, the Vietnamese were hustling to find new prisons. In addition to the Hilton, we gave the various POW camps names like Skid Row and the Plantation. They opened a new complex that had once been a French film studio. It was farther out on the outskirts of Hanoi than the Hilton. We called it the Zoo. It was there that I was moved with Ev right after being tortured at Heartbreak.

The Zoo housed over 100 POWs. It had a swimming pool in the middle of the several large one-story rectangular buildings. The pool was full of stale water, garbage and bugs—a bad-smelling, mosquito-breeding site. Since the Zoo was not originally a prison, most of the rooms (now cells) had a window. But the Vietnamese didn't want communication between the POWs, and soon after we arrived, our guards became bricklayers. They bricked up all windows to prevent us from seeing each other or using hand signals to communicate.

Within minutes of being put in with Jim and Ev and Jim's telling me that everyone who survived the horrendous Heartbreak interrogation went past name, rank, serial number, and date of birth, I heard a syncopated knock on our wall.

I already knew about the tap code. While in Heartbreak, I had learned about it from a POW named Fred Cherry, who was in the cell next to mine. Fred had been shot down in late 1965: He was a tough old-timer and knew the system. An African-American, who now weighed about 120 pounds, Fred was back in Heartbreak to be punished for having refused to make a propaganda tape. One day, when I was on the slab in stocks, I heard an-ever-so-quiet seven taps in the rhythm of "shave and a haircut—two bits." I had no idea who it was or what it meant. I made a few random taps back. "Shave and a haircut—two bits" came again. Once again I tapped several times. Fred knew that the new prisoners started out in Heartbreak, and, since I didn't give the right response (two taps), he knew I was a new guy who didn't know the code.

It was essential to know the tap code—at times it literally meant the difference between life and death. Fred Cherry, bless him, hollered from his cell to make sure I heard. He yelled, "Who are you?" I hollered back, "Major Leo Thorsness out of Takhli." "Okay, got your name. Now learn this tap code—organize the alphabet into a matrix of five rows, five letters in each row. Throw the K away so you have 25 letters. For a K, send a C, from the context of the word, you'll know if it's a K." He went on, "First tap the row, pause, then tap the column, pause before the next letter."

The guards heard Fred, of course—all of Heartbreak heard Fred. They came running and beat the hell out of him and put him into the stocks. But he had clued me into the tap code.

Visually it looks like this:

A	B	C	D	E
F	G	H	I	J
L	M	N	O	P
Q	R	S	T	U
V	W	X	Y	Z

Communications were our life blood. In practical terms, the tap code allowed us to get the names of the new shoot downs. And as soon as any POW learned the name of a new guy, like Fred did for me, it was spread throughout the camp. Then a POW would tell a Vietnamese interrogator that he knew that Leo Thorsness was alive and in Heartbreak. That meant another beating because it proved he had communicated. But we felt that if the North Vietnamese prison officials knew the other POWs knew, then the odds of the named POW disappearing went down.

Another reason communications were critical was to pass on news of the beginning of a new "purge." Every so often the prison officials were told by the North Vietnamese government to get propaganda from American POWs. The North Vietnamese believed that if officers in the United States Air Force and Navy condemned the war, it would help the antiwar movement turn America against the war. The North Vietnamese loved the antiwar movement. I had an interrogator tell me more than once: "We know we cannot defeat the United States military in the jungle, but we will defeat you in the streets of Washington, New York, and Los Angeles." As the years went by, they knew that the longer they hung in there, the better their chances were.

At the beginning of a purge, the Vietnamese picked a prisoner and told him to condemn the war by making a tape recording or writing a letter to the American government or memorizing a statement to be repeated to some visiting delegate. When that POW got back to his cell, after having been tortured for refusing to be a propaganda tool, he immediately went to the wall and began to tap. It was terrible news to know what might be coming, but, if you knew what they wanted, what the POW had done—what he said and how he said it—and why they finally stopped torturing him, the information might make the difference between living or dying during your own torture session.

When a guard wanted to check on us, or had something to give us, he used the flipper in our cell doors—an eye-level window about a foot long and eight inches tall with a hinge on the bottom. Frequently the guard would sneak along the outside walls of our cell blocks and, when he got to our flipper door, quickly yank it down in hopes of catching us tapping a message. We learned how to catch them by lying on the floor and eyeing the half-inch gap between the bottom of the door and the floor. If a guard was standing there, or sneaking up, we could usually see the soles of his shoes. When we knew there was no guard outside our cell door, we quietly tapped the first five beats of "shave and a haircut." The POW in the next cell would check under his door to make sure there were no guard shoes there, then come to the wall and tap twice—the end of the rhythm.

Of course it was an advantage if there were two or three in the cell. One would do the tapping, the other stay on the floor looking through the crack under the door. If a guard came, the POW "clearing" under the door would slap the floor. Hearing this, the POW tapping or listening on the wall would hit the wall with the butt of his clenched fist, making a thumping sound that stopped communications instantly.

Being caught usually meant a beating. Occasionally, instead of a beating, the prison guards made us kneel as a punishment. To kneel while having to hold your hands above your head may not sound difficult or painful. But try it on rough concrete for an hour or so with bare knees. Keep trying until you no longer can keep your arms up, then until your back gives out. Forced kneeling is a long, slow, and increasingly painful punishment.

Most nights, especially when in solitary, we would tap to the POW in the next cell "GBU"—*God bless you*. Those three letters were tapped like this: G is second row, second letter so tap ** **, slight pause, then B, * **, finally U, **** *****.

Tapping these faint percussions on the walls of our cell kept us human. They also were the key to our defiance.

———

One of the worst things about being tortured is not being able to fight back. But every once in a while, thanks largely to the tap code, we got in a lick or two. Soon after I was shot down, for instance, the Bertrand Russell War Crimes Tribunal was staged in Stockholm. Russell, the British peace activist and philosopher, was by then in his dotage, but he pulled together an international group of communists, pacifists, and antiwar fellow travelers whose common denominator was a hatred of America and a belief that North Vietnam was heaven on earth. Among those who testified against and judged us at the Tribunal were figures such as philosopher Jean-Paul Sartre, then in his Maoist phase; the Australian communist journalist Wilfred Burchett; Carl Oglesby of Students for a Democratic Society; the American pacifist David Dellinger; and Ngo Thi Nga, a teacher from North Vietnam.

The North Vietnamese government ordered the authorities at the Hanoi Hilton to obtain "confessions" from two POWs that could be presented to the War Crimes Tribunal. The torture was brutal. The two men chosen were Nels Tanner and Ross Terry, a two-man Navy crew. They were in solitary cells but with the tap code were able to make up similar stories. One fabricated story flattered the North Vietnamese air defense system. It made their defense look top notch, and they knew it would please those attending Russell's event.

Perhaps it was the simplicity and similarity of the concocted stories that made them seem believable. One story the POWs told was of a Lieutenant Clark Kent who was so fearful of the North Vietnamese flak that, shortly after launching from the carrier, he would dump his bombs on the coast and turn back for the safety of the Gulf of Tonkin.

The other Navy flyer told of a fellow pilot named Lieutenant Ben Casey—from the popular eponymous medical drama on television—who launched with the others, crossed the shore line, but was too scared to fly over defended areas or to his target. Instead, he flew over rice paddies where there was no flak, dropped his bombs on remote foot paths in an open field, and used his afterburner a lot so as to run low on fuel in a few minutes and have to return to the carrier quickly.

Once the Vietnamese got these statements, the torture of the two POWs ended. The stories made it to the War Crimes Tribunal in Stockholm. They were entered into the record and received significant discussion until one of the Americans noted the names: Clark Kent and Ben Casey!

When the word got back to the camp, the two Navy flyers were tortured long and hard. Both were beaten and isolated. Ross spent 18 months in solitary with his arms handcuffed behind his back. Why? Because their fabricated stories caused the North Vietnamese to look foolish in the eyes of the international media attending the War Crimes Tribunal. The news spread throughout the camp quickly by tap code. We had embarrassed the America-haters meeting half a world away!

CHAPTER 6

A DAY IN THE LIFE OF

Days when you were not pulled into interrogation were days to look forward to. They had a routine centered around a wake-up gong, emptying your rusty bucket (toilet) into a sewer line, getting two thin meals and three daily cigarettes.

Time loses its shape and meaning in prison. Aviators' pride and joy are accurate watches they can "hack" (synchronize) each morning at the general briefing. These were lost during ejection or taken by the North Vietnamese, but the obsession with the clock remained. Many of us wondered constantly what time it was and tried to synchronize the passing hours to the prison's gongs.

Most POWs were able to keep their wedding rings until they arrived at the Hanoi Hilton, where, if not given up voluntarily, they were pulled off by the guards. Mine was a simple white gold band that had only once been off in the 14 years Gaylee and I had been married—during surgery. I felt it was worth a fight. After knocking me down, two guards forced my fist open but still could not remove the ring, which had grown into my finger. A short time later another guard came into the interrogation room with a large knife and said, "You give the ring, or you give the finger." With as much courage as I could muster I said, "I keep my ring."

I won very few battles as a POW, but this was one of them. We have now been married for 53 years, and I still have my wedding band and all ten fingers.

The morning gong sounded around 6 a.m. About an hour later a guard would open the flipper in the cell door. Typically, he handed over three cigarettes to each man in the cell. After the extreme brutality, this was the last thing I had expected. I got more cigarettes each day than meals. The guard had a "punk" with him to light a cigarette. The punk was a long piece of toilet paper that looked like a quarter-inch piece of rope; it was rolled so tightly that it burnt slowly with a live ember at the end. If you were "good," the guard appeared again at noon and again in the early evening with the punk so you could smoke all three of your cigarettes.

Smoking was a big deal for the guards, who were almost all nicotine fiends. There were times when a torture session was suspended, and the POW was allowed to smoke a cigarette because the guards wanted to take a break and light up themselves. Smoking became something of a fetish for us, too. On those occasions when I had a non-smoking cellmate, I would get him to take his three cigarettes and then give them to me. I smoked two cigarettes each time the punk came around, lighting one off the other.

————

There were one or two guards who showed their humanity. One of them in particular would occasionally talk to us in sign language while one of his friends watched as a lookout. He showed us a scar he apparently received from a U.S. attack while driving a truck in the south. We taught him to count to ten in English and he taught us to count to ten in Vietnamese. I'd probably buy him a beer if I ran into him today.

For the most part, however, we would have gladly killed our guards. Many of the POWs stay in touch today by email and sometimes reminisce in staccato communiqués about the guards— ill tempered, sometimes vicious men to whom we gave names like Bug, McGoo, Mr. Blue, Frenchy (because of his accent), Hollywood (because he wore dark glasses), Pox (because of his pitted face), and the Soft Soap Fairy (who usually played the good cop in interrogations).

We were on constant alert for their defining characteristics. Usually these had to do with their violent relationship to us. But sometimes their own strange proclivities came into play. One day, for instance, my future cellmate Mike Christian heard the desperate squawking of a duck. He and others in his cell immediately took turns looking through a peep hole in the bricked-up window. There was a guard avidly having sex with this desperate creature, who became known to us as Darla the Duck. Another of the POWs, Jim Warner, reminded me recently of a guard who was caught in flagrante with a dog. Afterwards Jim and his cellmates would occasionally make the sounds of a dog in distress, knowing that the guard would frantically run toward the noise. He became known as Sniffles the Pooch Puncher.

However we caricatured them, we couldn't make the guards human because they had given themselves over to the system they served. Most were unemotional, skillful torturers who have left their indelible signatures on all our bodies and who still appear now and then in our dreams.

CHAPTER 7

DINNERTIME

We each had a short, curve-handled aluminum spoon and a small porcelain pitcher, which a guard came around twice a day to fill with boiled water. It was not enough, especially during the hot summers. One can get past hunger rather quickly. It comes on, and, if no food is available, moves away. Thirst never leaves. Keeping a pebble in my mouth helped—a trick learned in Boy Scouts.

The food was bad. Back home people made jokes about fish heads and rice. We would have counted ourselves lucky to have had fish heads. We all lost significant weight within a few months. Some of the longest-term prisoners developed blind spots in their vision because of poor nutrition. We were fed twice a day, 9 a.m. and 4:30 p.m. Both meals were the same: a bowl of green weed soup, as we called it (boiled greens with no seasoning), and a saucer of steamed rice filled with debris.

The guards bringing meals carried two buckets—one with the green weed soup and one with the rice—on the ends of a shoulder board. After dishing up the paltry portion, the guard opened the door to hand it out. When we heard the keys in the lock, we had to line up facing the door. When the door opened, even if it was the lowest ranking guard, we had to make a full bow. If you refused to bow, or bowed wrong, it meant a beating. The same routine had to be followed each time the door closed. Occasionally one soup bowl was fuller than the others, or one saucer had more rice. To make it fair, we rotated who was first, second and last served for each meal.

The monotony of the food made eating mechanical. But then, late in 1967, when I had been in the cell at the Zoo with Jim and Ev for about six months, we received what we grandly called the "third dish." This was a truly big event. We speculated on the reasons they were giving us more food. Could it be that they were trying to fatten us up because we were going home soon?

The third dish was a sort of mystery food that led to more speculation. It was a whitish color, firm in texture, and cut into half to one-inch chunks, which were covered with a greenish thick liquid. We each had opinions about what it was. We speculated before, while, and after we ate it. Each proposal was summarily dismissed by the others. Finally I had an "ah ha" moment and said that I knew exactly what it was. Ev, who considered himself more of a gourmand than Jim, said, "Go ahead, Leo, make another dumb suggestion."

I gave him my opinion: "Green bananas cut into exotic pieces covered with béarnaise sauce."

Ev exploded, "That's the dumbest idea of all—there is absolutely no way that it is banana." He added, "Leo, I'll bet you a thousand to one drinks it is not bananas."

Looking at Jim, I said, "You witness this," as Ev and I shook.

Fast forward two years: Jim, Ev, and I had long been separated and moved to other cells, but we were still at the Zoo. Ev had been to an interrogation. As the guard escorted him back to his cell they went by the walled cooking area. A door was standing ajar and even though he was hurting badly, Ev looked in. To his surprise, he saw someone cutting bananas. The next day we were served that same "green bananas cut into exotic pieces covered with French béarnaise sauce." It took a couple of weeks for his tap code message to arrive from one cellblock to another: "LT fm ES, would you accept 500 banana daiquiris?"

Ev now lives in San Diego, and we live in Tucson. We see each other about every two years. Whenever I see him, at whatever time of day, if I want a drink or not, I order a banana daiquiri. So far I've had eight, but I plan on getting the remaining 492 I have coming to me.

After a meal, the guard returned, and we put our bowl and

saucer on the bench outside the cell door. Generally while the door was opened in the morning, we got to empty our toilet buckets. The bucket was usually rusty and often did not have a lid or had one that didn't fit. (Living with the stench of your own urine and feces was itself a form of soft brutality.) Our sandals were made from old rubber tires. The soles were part of the heavy tread and the straps over the top of the foot were from the inner tubes. It was a big discovery when you found you could also use them as cushioning on the bucket. You carefully placed one sandal on each side of the bucket—holding on to each as you sat down for a bowel movement. Sometimes when you got up, one of the sandals would slip out of your fingers and plop into the bucket—it happened to each POW at least once.

Most days "camp radio" was broadcast from the headquarters building, which had a mike, radio feed, and tape deck to play recorded material. When the camp radio played, the guards would come around and make sure we were listening.

The junk on the camp radio was either propaganda or the exaggerations that passed for news. If the story was about Vietnam, it usually involved their glorious victories over the "Yankee air pirates"—how they decimated and seriously destroyed (their words) an entire company or battalion or regiment of the American forces in South Vietnam, etc.

Exaggeration was also the norm when news of the United States came over the radio. Gaylee was from South Dakota, and I had been there enough from neighboring Minnesota to be familiar with Rapid City. There was an exceptionally large rainstorm in 1972, which burst a dam in Rapid City. Unfortunately about 200 people were killed. The camp radio mentioned the event, claiming that the criminal capitalist construction had been responsible for the disaster, which had killed over 2,000 people. Exaggeration by a factor of ten or more was normal on the camp radio.

CHAPTER 8

BAD MEDICINE

Medical care in the prison was almost nonexistent. A few POWs got a cast for a badly broken arm or leg. But for most of us the only treatment was perseverance. The insides of my knees were torn up; I figured out how to walk pigeon-toed so the pressure was on the outside of my knees and I could move. Others were far worse off than I was. A couple of POWs had only one working leg. For them, the Vietnamese provided a crutch.

No POW was missing an arm or leg. In the early years that was a subject of much discussion by tap code. Later, when we were together in larger cells, we had that same conversation by voice. We wondered, we hoped, that there might be a separate amputee camp. We knew that when people pull negative "Gs" while ejecting from a speeding aircraft arms or legs are occasionally severed. Certainly some of the pilots who suffered these injuries must have made it to the ground alive. Eventually, after piecing together the various POWs' injury stories, including what POWs knew about their crew members, we figured out why there were no amputees in camp: those missing an arm or leg, or suffering other life-threatening injuries, were tortured for what information they might have, then left to die.

Bill Metzger, a strong young naval aviator, helped substantiate this theory. During ejection his right leg was mangled, resulting in a three-inch femur overlap. They interrogated him near where he landed outside Hanoi. When they finished the interrogation, they left him outside for two days. But he was too tough to die. He lived with the three-inch overlap until back home at Bethesda hospital.

There they medically salvaged one inch of three-inch overlap in the right leg, and cut two inches out of his left leg.

———

According to the old timers in the camp—those shot down in 1965 and 1966—the summer of 1967, my first in prison, was especially hot. With the windows bricked up, the air didn't move and the cells just got hotter and hotter. After sundown the concrete seemed to radiate the heat it soaked up during the long days, so there was little temperature relief at night.

At the end of the cellblock was a room with a water faucet. Every four or five days we were taken to the room. A rubber bucket was the only thing there. We were not allowed much time, and the water ran slowly. At best, we got maybe a half bucket each to pour over ourselves. That was our bath.

Most of us were fathers with children, and, having had small children in an era before servicemen had air conditioning in their homes, we were familiar with heat rash. Little babies would break out where skin touched skin: inside their arms at the elbow joint, under their arms by the armpit, and between the cheeks of the buttocks. In the hot summer prison days in 1967, with poor and inadequate food, not enough water to drink, and baths rare, our skin got the same problem in the same places, except that in Hanoi it was skin rash on steroids.

One day I noticed a small lump in a rash area near my groin. By the next day it was larger and sorer. Within a couple more days I found a couple more tender lumps. Soon the groin lump developed a "head." It was a boil. Once a boil developed a head and broke, because we did not have soap and water to clean the area, the drainage infected other areas of the body. Soon more boils developed. The boils eventually became carbuncles, which continued to enlarge. Eventually I had so many boils and carbuncles that it was nearly impossible to sit or lie down without significant pain.

According to the tap code, a lot of POWs had the same problem. We learned there was a relationship between skin pigment and the number of boils: the darker the skin, the fewer the boils. As I recall, Fred Cherry, the African-American pilot who had taught me the tap code in Heartbreak, had none. I tapped to him one day, "Sure, you black guys get all the breaks."

Having too much time on our hands, someone came up with the idea of having a "boil contest." We decided to expand the boil contest to other cellblocks by using a visual format of the tap code. This required a line of sight between the cellblocks from two peep holes with a POW at each peep hole at the same time. We also needed POWs in each cellblock "clearing" so guards would not catch us communicating. Finally, we needed something to slide in and out under the door so the other cellblock could see. The best thing for that was toilet paper.

A couple of times a week, or less, a guard would come around with large sheets of very coarse toilet paper. The sheets were about 10 by 20 inches. The paper went from thick, where you could see the wood fibers, to gossamer thin. We would tear the paper into squares about three by four inches. The bigger each "wipe" the fewer wipes you had. There was no certainty when you would get more toilet paper. If you used all you had, you made do without.

Visual code was slower than the tap code simply because it took longer to slide a piece of paper back and forth than it did to tap your knuckle on the wall. To send an L, for example: three taps, hesitate, one tap. To send an L, one slid the paper back and forth so that it was visible, then not visible, three times, hesitate, then one time. Sight took about twice as long as sound.

It took a couple of weeks to collect the boil contest count from each cellblock. First each cellblock collected the numbers for the POWs in that cellblock. Then, when all the conditions were right, the data was sent from one cellbock to the next. We designated which cell in which block was the collection point for the data. The final tally took a couple of weeks, and the winner was Ed. (Because he may not want to be known as the boil champion of the Hanoi Hilton after all these years, I'm omitting his last name.) Ed was a very light-skinned man. The average was between 20 and 40 boils per POW. (Ever the middle American, I had 33.) Ed, the poor guy, had 243.

Exercise was a part of every POW's day and an expression of his creativity. How we exercised depended on the space in the cell, and our physical condition. Ray Vohden's foot was attached by just a two-inch piece of bone and flesh in his lower calf; he did upper body exercises. My knees were badly damaged, so I learned how to walk again—awkwardly.

Having no exercise equipment, we found ways to use what we had. For example, we usually had a one-by-two-foot towel. For arm strength and muscle tension, we rolled the towel lengthwise to make a "rope." By holding each end and pulling in opposite directions—in front or behind one's back—we had a good arm and shoulder exercise. For the POWs who had good arms and backs, push-ups and sit-ups were standard. Contests were held via the tap code to see who could do the most. Sometimes the number seemed extreme. But who could tell if someone in solitary was exaggerating?

To exercise my leg muscles, I stood on one foot, touching the wall for balance, and raised myself up and down on tiptoes 50 times for each foot several times a day. I exercised my shoulders and arms with my towel or pajamas. I would do a few push-ups, using the edge of the bed slab rather than the floor because it was easier on my back. Back injuries from torture ruled out sit-ups.

Back injuries were common among the POWs as a result of ejection and the torture—mine was from torture. As the prison years rolled on, my back pain grew worse, especially while standing or walking. In the big cell we slept on three-by-six-foot bedboards—planks nailed together. I found a way to prop up one end of the board about a foot. If I lay head down with my feet tied to the high end, my back pain was lessened.

When I walked, my back was crooked to the left significantly. Maybe because of how I looked while walking, I was able to scrounge part of a discarded blanket and fashioned a sling, and a short strap. I tied one end of the strap to the blanket sling and the other to the window bars. By slipping into the sling and hanging by my armpits, I was able to really stretch my back. It relieved the pain, and I spent a lot of "sling time." My POW friends enjoyed repeating, "Yep. There's Leo, just hanging around as usual."

When I finally came home, I had back surgery. A doctor known as the best back surgeon in Seattle showed me my x-rays. He said, "Look at this, your back has been broken here, and here, and here, and maybe here—three times for sure, maybe four." He went on about my bad shoulders and knees. Then a question: "Do you have good insurance?"

"Yes I do," I responded.

He smiled: "If you stay in Seattle, I'll make a million dollars off you."

———

Military aviators have good dental care, and we all went to prison with good teeth. We came home with bad ones.

Many of our dental problems were caused by the debris in the rice we were fed. No matter how painstakingly I inspected my rice, it was impossible to find all the grit and pebbles. Some POWs claimed the North Vietnamese added the little stones to the rice. We never knew for sure. But the problem was significant. When you hit a pebble chewing rice, a filling was often knocked loose, or a tooth chipped. You found a new part of your mouth to chew the rice; eventually a pebble discovered that part too. I learned to gum my rice to avoid the impact.

Like most of the others, I developed cavities—mainly from fillings that came loose after biting a pebble in the rice. If the cavity was open to the nerve, touching it or breathing air over it often caused a "flash" pain. We had no material to craft temporary fillings. But after we were put into the large cells, we occasionally got bread instead of rice. It was filled with weevils, but not with pebbles. One of the first times we had bread, a piece stuck in one of my cavities. I started to try to pry it out, but then realized that the tooth nerve was less sensitive with the bread in. Several of us began using "bread fillings."

We had many discussions about our teeth. During ejection, capture, or torture, a lot of POWs had teeth knocked out or broken. In prison we were given a toothbrush and occasionally a small tube of toothpaste. The brush soon lost its bristles and the toothpaste, even used sparingly, did not last long. Without care, as time went on, teeth with cavities or which had become loosened became worse. We wanted to keep our teeth no matter how bad they got, thinking that they could be saved when we got home. Some teeth, however, became so bad and painful that even we knew they were beyond salvation. None of us knew dentistry, and we could not get the Vietnamese to give us a pliers or some other tool to pull them. Most of us, however, knew that an abscessed tooth is an infection at the tooth's root, or in the gum next to the infected tooth. If the abscess was in the gum, the swelling from the pus was obvious.

The last couple of years, when we had been moved into the big cells, we were allowed to take a bath every other day, going to a concrete tank near the cell door and using a rubber bucket to pour water over ourselves. The water drained into a shallow gutter that ran by the tank, under the prison wall and into the Hanoi system. One day a POW spotted a tiny box just under the water in the gutter. When the guard was not looking, he snatched it up and managed to get it into the cell. It was a phenomenal find. Inside, neatly packed in grease, were more than 50 razor blades—the old-fashioned ones used in a safety razor. The toilet in these large cells was a "squat hole." We devised a way to secure and hide the razor-blade box just out of sight of the hole underneath the cement squat slab.

We had an instant and important use for the razor blades: to cut a slit in our gums so the pus could drain. It was a foul-tasting mess, but pure relief when the pressure was released.

I had a unique and somewhat humorous dental experience a couple of months before we were released in early 1973. The nightly "Christmas Bombings" of Hanoi in 1972 by our B-52s had convinced the North Vietnamese to begin serious negotiations to end the war. They started trying to burnish their image as captors, both with the outside world and even with us. They announced one day that a dentist was coming to the camp. We were all a bit skeptical, but I had several bad cavities causing varying degrees of pain and accepted the offer.

When the dentist arrived a few days later, three of us were taken to a familiar small building—the one used for interrogations. Inside was the dentist sitting at an old-fashioned dental drill. The business end had a bit at the end of the handle. Between that and the pulley were the two lines that rotated the bit. From the pulley downward were lines that were attached to the foot pedal. My first memory of going to the dentist dates back to 1937 when I was five. Even then, the dentist in Westbrook, Minnesota, did not turn the drill with a foot pedal.

I was directed to sit in the chair. My cavities were obvious to the dentist as he looked in my mouth. He stuck the drill in my mouth. The bit turned slowly—more like grinding than drilling. This went on for a couple of minutes; no anesthetics of course. In his most professional way, he held the bit up toward the light. Sure enough, there was some cavity debris on it. Wanting to keep things sanitary, he wiped the bit—several times—on his pant leg. Then back to drilling. He smoothed out two cavities and said, "Finished."

I asked, "Any fillings?"

Rather indignantly he again said, "Finished."

Others had even better dental experiences. Swede Larson, who was shot down six days after I was, told this story:

> Two months after I arrived (July '67), I got my first rice. I was
> not aware of the stones the guards put in the rice at that time.
> I crunched down big time and badly fractured a molar. The big
> piece did not come out until it rotted badly in '69. In the fall
> of 1970, while living with Robby, the tooth really bothered me.
> The V [Vietnamese] cuffed and blindfolded me late one night,
> and took me to a hospital. A squat woman dentist in uniform
> sat me in a dentist chair and badly crushed my tooth with pliers
> while trying to extract it. She then grabbed an awl and tried for
> a long time to pry out the many pieces, while resting the shaft
> of the awl on top of my lip. Needless to say, she cut through
> my lip in several places while prying. Somewhere during the
> procedure, I passed out. My PJs were soaking wet and I was
> shaking like a leaf in late fall. As you would imagine, I did not
> get any anesthetic at any time. She never said a word to me the
> entire time. When I staggered out of the chair, she said to me
> in excellent English, "Your pain threshold is very low!"

CHAPTER 9

WALKING HOME

In my nearly six years in prison, not a day went by when I didn't think about and hope for freedom. I daydreamed about it, and I night-dreamed about it. I dreamed about it in the indistinct moments that separate sleep and waking. I dreamed about the physical sensation of freedom: how it felt on the body. I dreamed about how freedom might happen: by a daring rescue, by the military defeat of North Vietnam, by a POW exchange. These dreams sustained me for a time, but then, gradually, they stopped satisfying. I needed to do something. So one day I came up with a plan to walk to freedom.

It was 1968 and I had been moved to a cell with two other POWs: Chuck Tyler and Don "Digger" O'Dell. Chuck was a fountain of sanguine sayings. He was from Globe, Arizona, and told great stories in his "Tennessee Ernie Ford" style. He kept Digger and me laughing. Digger was quieter than Chuck, but a strong POW. He was from Michigan and had been an avid hunter and fisherman. We shared a lot of fun hunting and fishing stories, though Digger's were better than mine.

Our cell was about 11 by 11 feet. We talked in a very low voice because if the guards heard any sound it meant a beating. There was no window, no communication with other POWs except by our tap code. So we only had each other. Depending on how we felt at any given moment, we did various exercises—sit-ups, push-ups. The North Vietnamese, for whatever reason, told us we could not exercise. We did it anyway, knowing that the better shape we were in, the less vulnerable we would be to disease.

Occasionally a guard took us a short distance from the cell to a small area where an open well was surrounded by high walls. Instead of a faucet with a slimy floor under it—what I had experienced in the last cellblock—there was a cistern. This was much better when every few days we got to bathe. We dropped a bucket down the cistern, pulled up water, and poured it on ourselves. It felt very good in the summer and very cold in the winter.

Going back to the cell one day, we spotted a curled-up piece of 35-millimeter film on the ground. We planned how to get the filmstrip the next time we went to the bath area. The plan was simple: We would spread out so the guard could not watch each of us closely. Whoever was walking ahead would stumble and fall, slowly getting up. The guard would go to the fallen POW to whack him for being clumsy, giving the last guy in line a chance to snatch the filmstrip and stuff it in his pajamas. It worked.

Americans like inches, not millimeters. We converted the 35 millimeters to 1.38 inches. Then, using a homemade bamboo needle and thread pulled from my blanket, we made a nearly invisible stitch at each inch in our pajama drawstring. Now we had a tape measure. I lightly etched each inch into the edge of my wood-plank bed with a rusty nail, another stolen treasure.

With our tap code, we spread the word about the tape measure. We usually had two sets of pajamas. We would rinse out a set periodically and hang them on the bath area wall until our next bath a few days later. POWs from other cells used the same bath area. With a bit of stealth, other POWs swapped pajama strings with us and made their own tape measures. Operation Swap Pajama Strings spread throughout the camp. Soon we were all measuring everything that didn't move. Once we had a contest to see whose eyes were the closest—most narrowly set. The next contest was, of course, whose eyes were the farthest apart. We also studied how much the left and right hand varies by measuring the distance from the tip of our little finger to the tip of our thumb.

Once we had the tape measure, of course, we measured exactly how far it was around the open area in our cell. Our cell was 11 by 11 feet. We had three plank beds—two feet nine inches wide and six feet long—set on three brick stanchions 15 inches high, leaving about 16 inches between the beds. At the end of the beds was a space just over five by 11 feet. A two-by-four-foot hole on one end of the floor left an area of just over eight feet long and five feet wide. That was our walking track. With the tape measure we accurately measured the exact path we'd walk in this little track. It turned out that one lap was 23.4 feet. We next wondered how many laps to make a mile: 5,280 feet divided by 23.4 = 225 laps per mile.

To any American, the next question was obvious: How far could we walk in a day? We kept track. Each day we set our goal higher. Within a week we were walking ten miles daily. We set up a pattern in which one of us would lead for a mile, then the next would take the lead for a mile, then the third, and so on. Whoever was in the lead was also the counter. We soon learned to change directions every 25 laps to prevent dizziness. Using the camp's gongs, we computed we were walking about 1.75 miles an hour. If we were healthy enough, and not at interrogation, we could make ten miles in just under seven hours!

I knew that Vietnam was 10,000 miles from the United States and began thinking about this distance that separated me from freedom and the people I loved. We had decided not to walk on Sunday out of respect for the Lord. So if I stayed healthy and had no long interrogations, I could make sixty miles a week. Ten thousand divided by sixty is 166.6 weeks: 3.2 years. So I began to walk home.

The more I thought about it, the more real it became. If I really did walk 10,000 miles in that cell, somehow . . . some way . . . freedom would be mine at the end. I explained the idea to my cellmates; they agreed. I became so convinced that I would get home in 3.2 years that, if I were sick or being tortured and the other two POWs walked their ten miles, I got half mad at them because they would get home before I did!

When I finished ten miles I was euphoric. Often at night I reviewed my plan and recommitted myself to the effort required to walk halfway around the world to freedom.

Those I've told this story to usually have the same question: "Did you actually walk 10,000 miles?" The answer is that a year after I started my trek, I was moved to solitary confinement in another prison. The cell was only five and a half by six feet. It was not possible to walk, only to turn. In the one year I was in the larger cell, however, I walked 3,000 miles—about a third of the way home. I had made a cerebral escape and was closer to freedom in every way at the end of this time than I had been when I began.

CHAPTER 10

THE MEDAL OF HONOR

It was the summer of 1969, about two years after I was shot down, that I received an unusual tap code message. It had made its way slowly to the Zoo through a dozen cells in three different buildings to reach me. Like all messages, it was abbreviated and came through as: "LT U NOMINATED 4 MOH." I was the only POW with these initials so it had to be me.

One of the laws that ruled our lives was the more famous the prisoner the more torture he received. Had the Vietnamese discovered that Leo Thorsness was up for the Medal of Honor that would have been bad news for me. All the POWs knew this, and they were very careful not to let the message be intercepted.

As I later found out, recipients of the Medal of Honor must meet the following criteria: The actions for which they're honored must have at least two witnesses and the actions must be "above and beyond" the call of duty at the risk of their lives. "Above and beyond" means that if the serviceman had not undertaken the action that led to his nomination, there would have been no criticism.

There is always an enormous amount of research and documentation behind a nomination for a Medal of Honor. The person who had taken the lead in making the case for me was Bill Sparks, a fellow Wild Weasel who had served with me at Takhli Air Base. Bill was a good pilot; he was a lucky one too, since he completed his 100 missions and was rotated back to the States. Before he left, he told another pilot, Jim Clements, that he was doing the Medal of Honor research on me, although at that time there was no word whether I was a prisoner or had been killed in action. Some months later, Jim too was shot down and ended up in the Zoo. When he learned that I was there too, he initiated the tap code message that finally got to the wall of my cell.

It is sometimes said that character is doing the right thing when no one is looking. Something similar is true about the Medal of Honor. There have been countless cases of extreme bravery in combat that didn't have the requisite two witnesses to qualify for the Medal of Honor. Receiving it is sometimes a case of ending up in the wrong place at the wrong time and simply having to summon the courage to survive. Sometimes you are the only one who can save another's life and, as Hillel said, it becomes a matter of "If not me, who? If not now, when?"

When it comes down to it, almost every Medal of Honor recipient will say, "Look, I was just doing my job." That was certainly true with me, as I described in the opening chapter of this book.

As I discovered later on, my Medal of Honor took a twisted path in getting to me. After about a year of research and authentication of the recommendation, the nomination was confirmed and sent to the president in 1969. At that point it was not known whether I was dead or alive. Awarding the Medal of Honor was put on hold until my status was confirmed. (If I had been confirmed as killed it would have been presented posthumously to my wife and family.) When it was discovered that I was a POW, the Air Force decided to keep the award secret for fear that making it public would lead to more torture.

Unlike the Medals of Honor awarded to Jim Stockdale and Bud Day after we were released in 1973, mine was not for actions in prison, but for a mission I flew 11 days before I was shot down. I later discovered that there were "discussions at the highest levels" about my Medal of Honor because during the POW years, seven of the more than 300 American prisoners had collaborated with the enemy. Was I one of them? If I had been one of the collaborators, it would be difficult for the public to separate conduct in combat from conduct in prison and would reflect badly on the Medal of Honor. So a decision was made to investigate my performance as a POW before making the award. After the process was completed, President Nixon placed the Medal of Honor around my neck at a White House ceremony in 1973. I was humbled not so much because the leader of our country was giving me this honor as because the men I served with had thought me worthy of receiving it. Every time I put it on, I know I'm wearing it for all those who were braver than I but never recognized and for all those who didn't come home.

CHAPTER 11

SOLO

One night I was hustled out of my cell in the Zoo, blindfolded in the yard, and tossed into the back of a truck. After a bumpy ride of perhaps half an hour, three sharp turns and a quick stop, the tailgate clunked down, and I was pulled out and led by my arm a short distance, around two corners. As we stopped, I heard keys opening a lock. They pushed me in, removed the blindfold, and locked the door. I was alone in the pitch dark. It was solitary confinement—solo, as we called it. I had arrived at Camp Punishment, also known as Skid Row, as a result of my refusal to bow, or bow correctly to my captors and make other signs of obeisance and for generally being (as they said) "non-cooperative."

I stood in the middle of the tiny cell and stretched out my arms and fingertips to touch the opposite walls. That's about six feet. I reached down and felt a plank bed slab. At least I wouldn't have to sleep on the floor. I carried my worldly possessions with me: a cup, a thin straw mat, another set of pajamas, a threadbare blanket, and my aluminum spoon.

I could hear other cell doors being opened, feet shuffling, and cell doors being locked. At least other POWs were being moved here also.

I was tired and hoped that I could sleep until daylight. I felt around the slab as I rolled out my mat on it. My hand ended up in human feces—some guard had crapped right on the bed slab. I scraped off as much as I could on the slab and cleaned off the rest on my other pajamas.

I prayed hard. "Lord, I need your help and your comfort. I pray you will provide me the physical and mental strength to endure and to someday be free and with my family. And Lord, I pray for my wife and daughter. Give them peace and comfort, and please let them know they are forever in my mind—Amen." Prayer would be a big part of my life in solitary.

A few hours later, a little light filtered in through a hole near the ceiling. The feces had mostly dried, and I pushed it into a corner. The plank bed slab of the tiny cell was about two and a half feet wide. That made the remainder—my "living room"—three by six feet. The door had a window about 12 inches square at eye level with six vertical bars about the size of the steel bars used in reinforcing concrete. There was a little swing door over the barred window that blocked most light. The ceiling was high, maybe ten feet. A light bulb hung on a twisted pair of electric wires. It was on.

The keys jingled, the lock turned, and the door opened. The guard made a choppy gesture and said, "Go office." He pointed to the way: a four-foot wide dirty walkway between the long low prison building and a high gray dirty wall topped by broken glass embedded in concrete. We walked by many more cell doors. As we rounded the corner I saw a dripping faucet feeding a mat of slime on the concrete below it. This was the "bath" area that I would get to use for a few minutes every four or five days. The guard pointed me toward a small low building maybe 20 by 20 feet. It was the "office," a nasty euphemism for the interrogation room.

Sitting behind the bare wooden table, the interrogator gestured toward a stool and simply said, "Sit." He started out being the "good cop," offering me a drink of water and appearing to be pleased that I accepted it. "Do you know the name of this prison camp?" he asked. I shook my head. He continued, "This is Camp Punishment. You are here because you do not follow our humane and lenient camp regulations." I tried to interject something, but he stepped on my sentence: "In this camp you will follow them or face severe punishment—do you understand?"

Over the years I had learned to say, "I understand your words," in these situations. Surprisingly, that response ended the interrogation, and I was escorted back to my cell.

As we returned, I caught a glimpse of the front of the prison building—low and narrow with cell doors just like on the back side. In front and midway down the building were a few cement blocks a couple of rows high in a circle—obviously a well with the bucket and attached rope sitting by the side.

Shortly after I was back in my cell the door opened. I was given a small pitcher, which the guard filled with warm water. He closed the door and, through the barred door window, handed me three cigarettes and the punk to light one. Later I would get a bucket "toilet" and the two standard meals: green weed soup and rice. Life in solitary had begun.

During the siesta between gongs, I lightly tapped the first five beats of "shave and a haircut" on the wall. In a couple of seconds I heard "tap tap." We quietly and carefully had a lengthy "comm" session tapping information and questions back and forth: names, what we thought was up, whether we knew the other POWs who came last night, and if we thought any of the guards or interrogators who enjoyed torturing us were here. My spirits lifted. I was in solitary but I wasn't alone. I shared walls with three comrades in arms: left, right, and behind.

My first communication session turned out to be with Bud Day, one of the toughest POWs in North Vietnam. Bud was from Sioux City, Iowa, only about 100 miles from where I was raised in Minnesota. We had a lot in common in terms of upbringing and careers in the Air Force. His story had become something of a legend: shot down and captured, a daring escape soon after, and a desperate journey of 11 days subsisting on frogs and roots as he tried to make his way south to safety. He was shot and captured within sight of the American line and brought to Hanoi, where his legend had grown by the maximum resistance he offered as a prisoner. Bud was the hardest of the hard men in the Hanoi Hilton. (He would be awarded the Medal of Honor for the bravery he displayed in captivity.) I felt lucky he was next door to me.

Bud had been shot down a few months after me and was the senior ranking officer (SRO) in most of the cells in which he lived. Being SRO was a bad thing. SROs are understood to be the tip of the POW spear in camps and are thus subjected to more brutality.

I had been at the Zoo for about a year in two different cells with two different sets of cellmates when I was moved into solo. I ended up spending a year at Camp Punishment. The treatment was less brutal than in my initial 18 days and nights of interrogation in Heartbreak, but the camp was accurately named. The North Vietnamese still wanted us to cough up material they could use in their propaganda efforts to condemn the United States as an evil and aggressive nation attacking a small peace-loving country. You knew it was bad news when you were taken to the "office" and saw a tape recorder or a tablet and pencil on the table. Those of us selected for Camp Punishment were told we were there because of our "noncooperative" attitude. We were beaten, forced to kneel on concrete, and tortured in other ways. Several times the interrogator told me, "You must learn to suffer."

This I had already done. I had learned also that suffering was more than physical pain. Time itself was an enemy. Each POW developed his own way of "passing time." Some mentally solved math problems. Others "wrote" poetry. (We had no pencils or paper, so writing was an act of memory as well as composition.) Several POWs designed houses. One became so enamored of his cerebral structure that he actually built the house he mentally designed in solitary once he got home. When I chatted with him some years later, however, he admitted that this structure, which had seemed so grand in a North Vietnamese prison, was not functional or pleasing to the eye, but he stayed in the house. He loved it because it had helped him defeat time in North Vietnam.

Most of my solo time was spent making plans for the future, reliving and in some cases reconfiguring memories of the past, and learning poetry via tap code from fellow POWs.

My plans always included a lot of family, faith, fun, and friends. (About flying, my fifth F, I was not so sure.) I worked hard that year to get a perspective on myself, the kind of thing you never bother to do when you don't have time on your hands. I was no longer sure of who I was. I knew I was not who I had been—that other self I carried with me through prison like a familiar stranger, someone I had once known well but had grown apart from. I saw an obvious truth about this fellow: He had been too involved in his work, flying all week and checking out a plane on weekends to increase his chances of promotion. He had forgotten what was really important in life. I think almost all POWs had a similar epiphany in solitary. I had loved being a fighter pilot, but I knew now that if I ever managed to get out of prison, I'd never again be able to put my nose to the grindstone and keep it there. I wasn't sure what type I now was, but I knew it would never again be type A.

Sitting alone in my five-by-six-foot cell, dealing with the time on my hands, I made plans for a future that might never arrive. My plans now all started with the same sentence, "Gaylee, if you think this is a good idea, maybe we should ..." It was not a formulation that the older version of myself with whom I shared this solitary cell would have used.

I had ejected at 600 knots injuring my legs, and my back had been seriously injured under torture, so I knew I would never again follow what had been my bliss: flying ejection-seat fighters. But I saw other possibilities. I had a good military record and was sure I could remain in the military as a non-aviator—maybe becoming the military attaché in a U.S. embassy.

Another option was to become an academic. I had gotten my bachelor's degree and a master of science. I could go back for a PhD. I would enjoy passing on the knowledge I had gained during my career: I had worked with truly outstanding men and women in the military. I understood combat and prison, and I had seen excellent leadership firsthand. Becoming an academic had been in the back of my mind even before I was shot down. I spent many days in solo dreaming about what courses I could teach, working up lesson plans, and imagining the class sessions.

A third option involved politics. Most people who run for office have never been without the freedom Americans are given by birthright or lived inside the communist system. I had firsthand experience of defending United States national policy in combat and prison. Most of our elected officials had neither. (I eventually tried this course for a time after my release, serving in the Washington state legislature and losing U.S. House of Representatives and Senate races in South Dakota by a few hundred votes.)

But however much you tell yourself that you will defeat solitary by looking forward and through mentally challenging plans and propositions, most of the time there involves memories. During my year in Camp Punishment, I recalled vividly—so vividly, in fact, it was more like reliving than simply remembering—experiences I had more or less forgotten. Like a job I'd had during high school summers working for a building contractor in Walnut Grove, Minnesota. It was hard work wheeling cement, carrying cement blocks, and putting up siding and shingles. Mostly I worked on barns and granaries. In solo, I mentally rebuilt a couple of barns. I remembered the dimensions and where we used two-by-sixs for rafters and joists and lots of one-by-tens as boards for siding and the hayloft floors. My challenge was to convert the different dimensions of lumber into square feet. I remembered the overhead costs and the cement costs for the foundations and was somewhat familiar with what lumber cost. I knew what the contractor charged the farmer for his barn. Knowing how many men worked on the barn and how long it took, I was able to figure the material and labor costs.

I recalled scouting experiences. When my family had moved to Walnut Grove, I started high school, and Boy Scouts became a passion. I worked my way from Tenderfoot to Eagle Scout. A particularly lively memory involved a ten-day canoe trip from Ely, Minnesota, into Canada with five canoes, ten scouts, and the guide. Some of the scouts had never been in a canoe, so we practiced the first morning, then loaded up after lunch, and pushed off. Each canoe had two persons except for the one I shared with a friend named Bud Schultz. We took the 11th person since we had some canoeing experience. Chuck, a high school friend, was our passenger. He was, in the parlance of the day, a "spaz." It was better to have him riding in the middle than paddling from the front or back where his lack of coordination could do us damage.

The lake we crossed into Canada was crystal clear. As we approached shore, we could easily see the rocks on the bottom through several feet of water. Bud and I slowed the canoe as we approached shore. The bow was maybe five feet from touching the bank when Chuck decided it was time to help out. He looked over the side, saw a nice flat boulder, and felt it was right to step over the side onto the boulder and help us get the canoe on shore. Lakes around Walnut Grove have gradual slopes. We measured later and Chuck had tried to step on a rock that was seven feet under water! Anyone who has ever been in a canoe knows what happened. The canoe flipped us and all the supplies into the lake. The first time I relived that memory while in solitary, I laughed out loud.

I spent a lot of time reviewing lists that I learned in grade school: presidents, state capitals, Great Lakes. Using the tap code with other POWs, I filled in the blanks in those lists that I couldn't remember. Like most kids, I had gone to Sunday school whether I wanted to or not. Part of Sunday school was memorizing Bible verses. As a POW, remembering those verses became important to me, and I learned others using the tap code. By the time we came home, nearly all of us knew the 23rd Psalm.

> The Lord *is* my shepherd; I shall not want.
> He maketh me to lie down in green pastures:
> He leadeth me beside the still waters.
> He restoreth my soul:
> He leadeth me in the paths of righteousness for his name's sake.
>
> Yea, though I walk through the valley of the shadow of death
> I will fear no evil: For thou *art* with me;
> Thy rod and thy staff, they comfort me.
> Thou preparest a table before me in the presence of mine enemies;
> Thou anointest my head with oil; my cup runneth over.
>
> Surely goodness and mercy shall follow me all the days of my life,
> and I will dwell in the house of the Lord forever.

During the really tough first couple of years in prison, I felt like the 23rd Psalm was dictated by the Lord specifically for POWs.

I decided to remember the 31 seniors who were in my small graduating class from Walnut Grove in 1950. At first I could remember only a few. But then I came up with some of the others by trying to remember whom I sat by in certain classes. Then a couple more popped up from my football, basketball, and baseball teams. A couple more were found by remembering the girls I had dated. At this point I could remember 17 names.

In prison I learned my dreams could be controlled by concentrating hard on a specific topic or subject while trying to fall asleep. So I told myself, "Find the other 14 classmates in your dreams." And I did—all but one. Shortly after I was released in 1973, my 1950 graduating class held a luncheon in Walnut Grove. I shared my experience of how I remembered all the names but one. I'm not brilliant, but I did not make the mistake of telling them which one I couldn't remember.

Using the tap code I memorized the poetry those around me knew. I lucked out and lived on the other side of the wall from a POW who knew all 96 lines of "The Ballad of East and West" by Rudyard Kipling. It took a long time to memorize. Once I forgot a line; I had only 95. You can imagine how long it took by tap code to find that dropped line.

Over the following few months, I lived next to POWs who knew other poems. Within six months I had memorized "Gunga Din" and "If" by Rudyard Kipling, "High Flight" by John Gillespie Magee, "In Flanders Fields" by John McCrae, "The Cremation of Sam McGee" by Robert Service, and "'Twas the Night Before Christmas" by Clement Clarke Moore.

Part of the memorization involved recitation. It was the only way to embed the poems firmly in my mind. I even worked on a good delivery, as if I were performing before a crowd. One day in the middle of "The Cremation of Sam McGee" the guard opened the door to give me my afternoon meal of soup and rice. I was half disgusted with him for interrupting me.

I made a commitment that when I was again free, I would study subjects I knew nothing about.

CHAPTER 12

THE QUESTION OF FREEDOM

Freedom is the most profound of subjects and also one of the hardest to say something profound about. As an American, freedom was handed to me at my birth, and I had taken that freedom for granted. A rusty nail helped me think about and understand freedom.

As I have said, we got a bath about once a week. The bath was at the end of the long building that comprised the 36 cells—two rows of 18—of Skid Row. It was not enclosed, just a faucet that dripped onto the accumulated slime of a concrete slab. On bath day, I was taken there by the guard, who hung around as I got a bit of water in the pail, splashed it on myself, and washed the best I could.

One day as I stood filling the pail, I noticed a rusty nail about four feet away just off the slab. I casually moved to that side of the slab as I splashed the water over my naked body. Intentionally I slipped a bit and while kneeling down got the nail in my hand and then in my shorts as I put them back on. Now I had a tool!

There were once windows in the solitary cells of Skid Row, but they had been bricked up. North Vietnam being a communist country, however, the mortar between the bricks was of poor quality. With my rusty nail and a lot of time, I slowly drilled a tiny peephole in the mortar. With my eye directly next to the hole, I could see a one-to-two-degree slice of the prison yard. When not peeking out, I plugged a bit of dirt in the hole so that the guard in charge of the cell could not tell that I could see outside.

I spent hours at that peephole. Now and then a POW walked by. The tap code allowed us to know and memorize the names of all POWs known to be alive in the system and to communicate with some of them. Very few, however, did we know by sight. Now, when a POW walked by my peephole on his way to interrogation, I would immediately start tapping to find out who he was. I could put a face together with a name.

One day a chicken hen with a flock of chicks walked past my peephole. For someone who had grown up on a farm, that was exciting. It brought a bit of normalcy to a sad place. It was big news to tap out the word that we had a hen and baby chicks in the camp.

A few days after the joy of seeing baby chicks, a guard walked through my view and an unexpected string of thoughts flashed through my mind. I imagined myself flipping a coin; reaching out, catching it, and slapping it on my hand. Heads it was! That meant the guard got tails. I won; he lost. The stakes of winning the imaginary coin flip were profound. My thought was this: Neither of us had any control over who our parents were. Had I gotten tails, my parents would have been North Vietnamese and his would have been American.

I kept watching out the peephole at this guard who had unfortunately lost the coin toss and spent hours comparing his life to mine. He was stuck living under a controlled system governed by brutality, not consent. He had very little chance to move up or even sideways in life, his freedoms were minimal and always conditional, and instead of having the right to open inquiry he was spoon fed only the information his government wanted him to know. He had nothing exciting or adventurous to look forward to; likely he would never visit another country or get a choice of whom to vote for. The more I thought about him and his life, the sorrier I felt for him.

By a figurative flip of a coin, I had been born a free American and he had been born a captive communist. Here I was, locked in a grimy, tiny five-by-six-foot cell, and he was walking around unrestrained outside. But I knew that I was the lucky one. In my 35 years of freedom, I had had a better, fuller life and had done and seen more than he ever would. A thought stuck in my mind that never left me in the years I was a prisoner: If I die now, I am way ahead of the game.

CHAPTER 13

BOREDOM

After a year or so in solitary I was moved into a small cell with Jack Bomar. We hit it off and faced together the POW's greatest enemy: boredom. We spent our days in a trance of memory and sometimes pain, waiting for something to awaken our attention.

To our utter amazement, and without the "camp radio" explaining why, the guard opened the flipper door one day and gave us a deck of playing cards. We were ecstatic if a bit suspicious. What was going on? Was this a trick of some kind?

The cards were Chinese-made, and thicker and less pliable than standard U.S. playing cards. We soon learned not to hold them long or firmly when it was hot because they absorbed sweat and became floppy. We played rummy and cribbage. The man in the cell on our left was in solitary. He told us by tap code that he too had cards and played solitaire every day. Soon he began tapping to us that he was winning about half the games he played. On the spur of the moment, I tapped, "Jim, are you cheating?" There was a long pause, then he tapped back, "Well, a little, it's more fun to win." Jack and I laughed and laughed. We gave Jim a very hard time with the tap code. But he kept cheating.

There were two POWs in the cell on our left. Both happened to be good bridge players. A few days after the cards were handed out, they tapped to us: "Jack and you know how to play bridge?" Jack was good, and I could play. "Yes, we know how to play bridge— too bad we can't get together a foursome."

The next day, they tapped to us, "We figured a way to play

bridge with two of us in each cell using the tap code." It seemed a bit far-fetched but we tapped back, "Let us know how."

The first problem to solve was how to randomly deal two decks of cards and have the same deals come out. Jim Bell, one of the POWs next door, developed the system. Set up the decks as they were when new: ace through king in each suit. Put the spades on the bottom, hearts next, then diamonds, and clubs. From the top, deal seven cards down in a row—left to right. Start over and put a second card on top of each of the first seven cards. Continue dealing and you will end up with three stacks of eight cards and four stacks of seven. On the cell wall, tap the stack number you want on the bottom—three taps for, say, number three stack. Next tap seven, then two—whatever sequence you want. Just put each stack on top of the last until all seven stacks are back into a whole deck. You now have two identical randomly arranged decks that can be dealt out.

Say that players North and South are in cell number one and that East and West are in cell number two. Let's say North starts the bidding at One Heart. The POW closest to the wall in cell one taps an H: two taps, pause, three taps (** ***). East, in cell two, passes: tap P (*** *****). South, in cell one, bids Two Hearts. Two taps (**), longer pause, then the H: (** ***). West, in cell two, bids Two Spades: two taps (**), longer pause, then S (**** ***). North bids Two No Trump: two taps (**), pause, then NT (*** *** **** ****). East passes: P (*** *****). South bids Three NT: (***) (*** *** **** ****). West Doubles: D (* ****). North, East, and South pass. P (*** *****). And so on.

It took perhaps ten times longer to play a hand than in normal bridge. But, what else did we have to do?

After about four months of bridge fever, they took the cards back with no more explanation than when they had given them. We looked for other obsessions.

———

Back when I was living with Chuck Tyler and Digger O'Dell, between our cell door and the bath area—some 50 feet away—were a

This photo was taken in 1963 at the Spangdahlem Air Base
in Germany. I still remember with joy the days as a young
fighter pilot preparing for a fate I had not yet discovered.

Harry Johnson and I, at this point mustachioed, striking a theatrical pose in a photo sent to our families from Takhli, Thailand early in 1967. By this time we had some 50-60 missions under our belts and were feeling pretty confident.

I learned a lot from my imprisonment, but will still always remember those days as the "bad old days." The first part of my captivity—this photo, taken in October 1967—was the worst.

President Richard Nixon awarded me the Medal of
Honor at the White House on 19 October, 1973. I was
blessed to have my family with me at the ceremony. On
my left, my mother Bernice Thorsness, my wife Gaylee, my brother John Thorsness, my daughter Dawn,
and my sister Donna Martinson.

Early in October 1974 I
visited President Ford at
the White House. I was in
a campaign for the U.S.
Senate against George
McGovern in South Da-
kota, which I lost by a
narrow margin.

Senator LEO K. THORSNESS, 11th District, King

My beautiful daughter Dawn at my desk
in the Washington state senate, 1990.

In 1983, artist Matthew Waki captured this moment
of my Medal of Honor flight as I skimmed over the
top of a MiG I just filled with 20mm holes from
my Gatling gun, April 19, 1967.

The "Zoo" at the Hanoi Hilton where I spent two years. Through the arch you can see the "Annex" in the background where I spent several weeks, 1993.

The door into cell 24 at the Hanoi Hilton. I was subjected to a lot of torture here. The same rat hole was there when I went back to look in 1993, just as I remembered it from the 1967 torture days.

When I returned to North Vietnam in 1993, I took Gay-lee with me so she could fill in the spaces created by my imprisonment. Here we stand at the entrance to "Heart-break," an evil place where the worst torture went on.

Here I am as a happy man in 1998, with the
two women in my life, Gaylee and Dawn.

few hot pepper plants. As we were escorted to the area, we noted that the plants had fruited and very slowly started growing peppers. We frequently talked about how those peppers, when they got bigger, would add flavor to our green weed soup. We worked endlessly on plans to steal them without being caught by the guards. And we had endless conversation about the peppers themselves. Were they hotter when small or when large and ripe? How much did they grow each week? How much would one pepper, if cut into thirds, affect the taste of the soup? The pepper caper taking shape in our minds passed a lot of time.

One day after the trip to and from the baths, Chuck declared, "They are big enough." Nodding, Digger added, "Yep, the next bath trip they are going down." I agreed, throwing in my two cents, "It's now or never. If we don't get 'em soon, the Vietnamese will."

The guard always followed the same routine: Unlock and open the cell door, line us up and make us bow, point to the bath area and fall in behind the three of us as we marched single file along the little path. Some bath days we were allowed to rinse out the pajamas we had worn for a week or more and then change into the clean set we carried to the bath. Our plan was that I would go first and have my clean pajamas in hand along with my towel. Chuck would follow me and Digger would be last in line. I would walk briskly and be next to the pepper plant, just 15 feet up the path, by the time Digger walked out the door. Just as Digger got out the door he would say, "*Boa coa*, towel." (*Boa coa* was the phrase we were supposed to use if we needed the attention of a guard.) Then, as he went back in the cell for his towel without waiting for permission, I would "accidentally" drop my pajamas, partly covering the pepper plant. As expected the guard stepped just inside the cell to see what Digger was doing, saying, "You stop—go bath!" Chuck stopped just behind me, blocking the guard's view of me, and I nabbed the peppers.

The pepper-napping worked perfectly! I had two good-sized peppers covered by my pajamas. The guard cussed out Digger but nothing more. We all ended up in the bath area behind the wall for a few minutes. Chuck and I rinsed our pajamas and hung them on the wall. As we walked back into the cell, Chuck and I each had a pepper cinched in our waistbands hidden by our pajama tops.

The second and last meal of the day arrived as usual at 4:30 that day. Making sure the guard was gone, we got our peppers from the hiding place. Using a spoon I cut both peppers into thirds. We each squished them and dropped our two pieces in the green weed soup. With the first spoonful we all nodded yes, we could taste the difference. There really was a slight "hot" spicy tinge, but the best part of the caper was that it had kept boredom at bay for nearly two weeks.

———

At about this time, the Vietnamese began to vary our diet. Occasionally, instead of green weed soup and rice they changed it to green weed soup and bread. The bread was French-loaf shaped, seven or eight inches long and two inches in diameter. It was a welcome change, and I've already described the effect it had on our dental woes.

I remembered my mother's flour bin. Like all farm wives in the 1930s and 1940s, she had baked our bread. I also remembered that sometimes weevils would invade Mom's flour. It would, of course, be thrown out. But the Vietnamese did not throw out weevil-infested flour. They baked the bread just the same.

As POWs we received no dairy products or meat. We were cadaverous and malnourished. There was no protein in green weed soup or rice. Some POWs spent a long time picking the weevils out one at a time while trying not to waste any bread. Some just ate them for nourishment. Weevils provided entertainment as well as protein. We came up with the idea of having a weevil contest. The next time we got bread, whoever had the most weevils won. A week later the bread came with the afternoon meal. We all took the contest seriously. The bread this time was very weevilly. Each of us wanted to win the contest, of course, and meticulously tore our loaf into very tiny pieces to make sure we found every weevil. After all results were in, the range was from 52 to 271. Turns out that I was again average: 121 weevils.

Chuck kept us entertained with one-liners. He generally started with the phrase "Just as my grandpa used to say ... " Digger and I would look at each other knowing full well we would question whether the saying really fit the situation and if his "grandpa" really said it. Sometimes we doubted that Chuck actually had a grandpa, or at least one that would say such odd things. We had a lot of discussion about Chuck's grandpa. Chuck always defended his grandpa as real and said someday we would meet him.

About once each six months, the POWs from one cell were taken out for a "work detail." It was great to be outside for a couple of hours. In my two years at the Zoo, I was on three work details, one of them while living with Chuck and Digger. A guard, one who spoke more English than most, unlocked the cell door in March 1968 and told us, "You work—you make plants grow."

Each POW had two pairs of pajamas, one t-shirt and one pair of shorts. The guard said, "Short," and we put on shorts and t-shirts. Outside the cell door were two empty pails just like our toilet pail in the cell. He motioned for us to follow him off the path into a small area, about 10 by 20 feet. The dirt had been turned and broken up. It had half-grown plants: pepper plants like the one we'd recently robbed and something that looked a bit like spinach. The guard then pointed to Digger: "You go bath get pail water—bring here." Digger went to the bath area, 40 feet away, dropped a bucket with the rope attached down the well about 15 feet, and drew up the water. When Digger brought the pail of water, the guard looked at me and pointed to the same open sewer where we poured our feces and urine each morning. With his best English, he said, "Go to sewer, bring half pail." All three of us being sharp Air Force majors, we got the picture: We were going to fertilize the plants with human waste.

The opening to the sewer line was about two and a half feet across. The level of sewage was two feet below ground level. I got down on both knees by the sewer edge, and put one hand on the ledge about a third of the way around the circle opening. I held the dirty rusty pail in my left hand, reached down, pushed some turds aside with the bottom of the pail, tilted it, and let it fill about half.

Dripping scummy stuff from the side and bottom, I carried it back to where Chuck, Digger, and the guard waited and watched. I set the pail on the ground next to the full pail of water. The guard, seeming satisfied that we were performing satisfactorily, looked at Digger and said, "Pour half water in shit pail."

After this was done, it was time for the high tech to kick in. The guard walked to the edge of the garden and picked up a sturdy stick about 18 inches long. He came back, handed it to Chuck and said: "You mix." Chuck took the stick, held it as close to the top as possible and gingerly stirred. It wasn't a good mix. The guard, unhappy, sternly told Chuck, "Mix hard." Chuck stirred a bit faster. More perturbed, the guard said, "Mix hard to bottom." There was about three inches of clearance between the top of the turds and Chuck's hand. Eventually the guard felt the turds were broken up enough and said, "Stop."

The guard nodded to me, the sewage carrier, and said, "Put by plants." I knew the odds were that I would not do it the "Vietnamese way." And I was right—I did it wrong. I didn't pour the right amount of turds and sewage by each plant, and I poured too close to the stem. By now, Chuck, Digger, and I were totally into it. Without saying anything, but with frequent eye contact, all three of us were finding this entire operation nearly unbelievable, a macabre combination of the humorous and the disgusting.

The process went on for another hour. Eventually we met North Vietnamese standards, breaking up the turds into the proper size and putting the right number of pieces the right distance from each plant. I only let the pail slip once. I caught it as it was slipping below the sewer surface—getting only one small turd between my hand and the edge of the pail. No matter how carefully I poured, some splashed on my feet, and Chuck's "stir hard to bottom" caused sewage to splash nearly to his elbow. Digger, the clean water carrier, escaped the slop. He was quite pleased with himself and later on enjoyed pointing this out to Chuck and me.

There was no question in our minds that when we finished our "shitty" job, we would get to clean up in the bath area. Digger got one last pail of water and poured half of it into my last half-full pail. As we finished the last plant, the guard looked at his wristwatch and said, "Finish. Go in. Go in." Chuck said, "We've got shit all over us, we must bathe." "No time," the guard replied. He looked at Digger's pail, half full, and said, "Use that water and go in—now!" Two other guards appeared from around the corner. We washed our hands the best we could, and quickly they locked us in.

We sat on our bed slabs and went back over the past couple of hours. Each of us, at least once said, "Can you believe what we just did?" Not surprisingly, Chuck had a saying to fit the occasion. He started, "You know, I just remembered something my grandpa always said." Digger glanced at me and said, "Get ready, Leo, here comes another one." Chuck said, "No this one is real—and it fits. My grandpa always said that 'If you stir shit long enough, you'll get some on you.'"

CHAPTER 14

PRISON SCIENCE

For the first three years, the prison officials did nothing special for holidays. The next couple of years they gave us an extra portion of food on Christmas. And the very last Christmas we were captives—Christmas, 1972—they gave us two whole cooked ducks, intestines and all. We ate around the innards. There were 28 POWs in the cell. Two scrawny ducks was not a lot—but it was a lot more than ever before. They were fattening us up.

In solitary, there was no real way to celebrate holidays except through memory. I recalled my good memories of each holiday as they came and went: Christmas, Easter, Thanksgiving, Fourth of July, birthdays, our anniversary. When I lived with other POWs, we each recalled and told of good times (never of bad times) and compared how our families celebrated holidays. On these special days you missed your family more than ever.

I arrived in Hanoi on May 1, 1967. My first holiday, July 4th, was a bad day: on my knees for being caught communicating. Thanksgiving came: green weed soup and rice. Christmas came: green weed soup and rice. A few months later, in the spring of 1968, Easter approached but we weren't sure of the date. Ev, Jim, and I all knew that Easter was related to the equinox and the moon, but we didn't know how. We remembered it generally fell in March or April.

With the tap code, we asked if anyone in our cellblock knew how to compute the Easter date. Sure enough, Jim Shively, on the far corner of the backside, said he had the formula. He claimed it was complex and did not offer to share it. He mentioned it would be difficult to specify the date because our windows were bricked up, and he could not see the moon. Jim was confident, however, that his "Easter computation" was better than anyone else's in the cellblock. He convinced us.

"Jim, when is Easter?" we continued to tap him. It was getting well into March, and he was still replying, "I'm working on it, don't worry." As best I remember, it was mid-April 1968 when Jim finally had the Easter date computed. With full confidence, he tapped, "Easter 1968 will fall on Sunday, May 12." There was a tap code uproar. None of us could remember Easter ever falling in May. But Jim tapped with self-assurance: "Yes, it is late this year, but that happens once in a great while."

Jim was a good guy, and so we accepted his assertion. Besides, we reasoned, what difference did it make? (Who knew that Easter is the first Sunday after the first full moon after the vernal equinox, and the vernal equinox always falls within a day of March 21?) We were confident the Lord would be pleased if we celebrated his resurrection on whatever date. And so it was, while the rest of the world celebrated Easter on April 14, 1968, we POWs celebrated it on May 12. Every Easter, I remember this and smile.

———

Another scientific question that obsessed us—primarily because we were being starved to death—was how much we weighed. I found out the answer when I was moved to a larger cell in a POW camp, built on the backside of the Zoo, that we called the Annex. We were eight POWs in an 18-by-18-foot cell. Attached to the outside of the cell was an eight-foot high brick wall surrounding an area 18 by 15 feet. The walled yard had a well, a squat-down toilet, and a small concrete tank. Twice a week we were allowed to stay in the outside area for about 30 minutes without the guard. We pulled water from the well and bathed, washed our extra set of pajamas, and got a little sun.

One day Bruce Hinckley said rather casually, "Well, let's see how much we weigh." Good idea. But how to do it? One of the POWs claimed that each inch lost around the waist equaled six pounds. With the tape measure, we measured our waist frequently.

None of us, however, had much confidence in this inexact and impressionistic formula.

Bruce said, "We have all the tools—tape measure, rectangular tank, and water."

The concrete tank in the courtyard was three feet high, three feet long, and 22 inches wide. If we scrunched ourselves into a ball, we could just fit into it. Our self-appointed weight expert said, "We will use Archimedes' Principle. You remember that, of course." Along with the other POWs I nodded knowingly and pretended that I knew what he was talking about. He gave us a quick review and the simple version of the principle: If you immerse a body in water, the body is buoyed up by a force equal to the weight of water displaced.

When the guard left, we quickly filled the tank with water. Bruce got in the tank and scrunched up so he wasn't touching the sides or bottom; the displaced water spilled out, and he got out. The tank was rectangular so we could fairly accurately measure the length, width and depth. We calculated the cubic inches displaced, converted them into cubic feet, multiplied by 62, the weight of one cubic foot of water. Bingo—we had our body weight.

A line of guys quickly formed to get into the tank. When my turn came, my body displaced 2.25 cubic feet. I weighed 135 pounds, about 40 pounds less than when I was shot down. The tap code was soon in high gear passing "Archimedes" around.

Pastimes such as the weight mania made the Annex a lively place. My stay there ended because of an escape. On the night of May 10, 1968, John Dramesi and Ed Atterberry got out through the roof of one of the cellblocks. They made it over the prison wall and into the Red River. They got four miles by daybreak, but couldn't find reeds or debris under which to hide. They were spotted by farmers, recaptured, and brought back to the Zoo. Then the punishment began. Ed was slowly tortured to death, but John somehow survived it all. The ranking officer in each cell was also brutally tortured for several days to extract information about any other escape plans. Over the next two months, torture was as constant and brutal as it ever got.

CHAPTER 15

THE LORD'S PRAYER

Sunday morning at the Hanoi Hilton was church time. To gather our "congregation," the Senior Ranking Officer (SRO) tapped "CC," quietly on his wall. Each cell in turn tapped "CC," and soon all have been alerted to Church Call. The service was a prayer and a reciting of Bible verses. If I was lucky, I was in a cell with one or two other POWs, and we could pool our knowledge of the Bible.

A failed rescue attempt led to the most memorable of our church experiences. It happened on November 20, 1970, when U.S. Special Forces staged a mission to rescue the POWs believed to be at Son Tay, one of the small prisons the North Vietnamese maintained outside Hanoi. The raid was brilliantly planned and executed perfectly. Our men landed at the prison in helicopters and came home without the loss of a single American. There was only one problem: all the POWs had been moved out of Son Tay about four months before the rescue effort so none of us went back with our rescuers.

The mission still turned out to be a huge success for us, however. Realizing that such rescue attempts could happen again, the North Vietnamese brought us in from outlying prison camps into the main Hoa Lo prison in Hanoi: the Hanoi Hilton. Within hours of the raid, we were moved into large cells—43 of us in my cell.

It was the greatest day of our prison life. For the first time, we were meeting POWs whose names we had memorized years earlier. Many of us had formed intense friendships through the tap code with men we'd never seen. As we met that night, "So this is what you look like" was heard over and over throughout the cell. We compared our treatment, and it seemed important to each of us to tell one another of our torture experiences. I've never seen more empathy in anyone's eyes than when telling a fellow POW about being tortured. We each needed to tell our torture story—once. We never told them again to the same POW.

The handshakes, back slapping, and bear hugs went on and on. Some of us had been tortured for the protection or benefit of a "tap-code buddy." Now there was love and respect to be repaid. No one slept that first night; too much joy, excitement, and talk.

The next morning, we needed to determine the SRO. The highest rank in our cell was O-4, which is a major. ("O" stands for officer, so O-1 is second lieutenant or ensign, O-2 first lieutenant, O-3 captain, O-4 major, O-5 lieutenant colonel, O-6 colonel, O-7 brigadier general, and on up to O-10 for a four-star general.) We put all the O-4s together and then compared the date when the rank was attained and arrived at a hierarchy. We did the same with the O-3s, the O-2s, and the O-1s. When we were done, all 43 of us knew exactly where we stood in the command structure. Our SRO turned out to be Ned Shuman—a really good Naval aviator.

The first Sunday in the large cell, someone said, "Let's have church service." Good idea, we all agreed. One POW volunteered to lead the service, and we started gathering in the other end of the long rectangular cell from the cell door. No sooner had we gathered than an English-speaking Vietnamese officer who worked as an interrogator burst into the cell with a dozen armed guards. Ned Shuman went to the officer and said there wouldn't be a problem; we were just going to have a short church service.

The response was unyielding: we were not allowed to gather into groups larger than three persons and we absolutely could not have a church service.

During the next few days we all grumbled that we should not have backed down in our intention to have a church service and ought to do it the coming Sunday. Toward the end of the week, Ned stepped forward and said, "Are we really committed to having church Sunday?"

There was a murmuring of assent throughout the cell.

Ned said, "No, I want to know person by person if you are really *committed* to holding church."

We all knew the implications of our answer: If we went ahead with the plan, some would pay the price—starting with Ned himself because he was the SRO. He went around the cell pointing to each of us individually. "Leo, are you committed?" "Yes." Ned then moved to Jim and asked the same question. "Yes," Jim responded. And so on until he had asked each of us by name.

When the 42nd man said yes, it was unanimous. We had 100 percent commitment to hold church next Sunday. At that instant, Ned knew he would end up in the torture cells at Heartbreak.

It was different from the previous Sunday. We now had a goal, and we were committed. We only needed to develop a plan.

Sunday morning came, and we knew they would be watching us again. Once more, we gathered in the far end of the cell. As soon as we moved together, the interrogator and guards burst through the door. Ned stepped forward and said there wouldn't be a problem: We were just going to hold a quiet ten-minute church service and then we would spread back out in the cell. As expected, they grabbed Ned and hauled him off to Heartbreak for torture.

Our plan unfolded. The second ranking man, the new SRO, stood, walked to the center of the cell and in a clear firm voice said, "Gentlemen," our signal to stand, "the Lord's Prayer." We got perhaps halfway through the prayer, when the guards grabbed the SRO and hauled him out the door toward Heartbreak.

As planned, the number three SRO stood, walked to the center of the cell, and said, "Gentlemen, the Lord's Prayer." We had gotten about to "Thy Kingdom come" before the guards grabbed him. Immediately, the number four SRO stood: "Gentlemen, the Lord's Prayer."

I have never heard five or six words of the Lord's Prayer—as far as we got before they seized him—recited so loudly, or so reverently. The interrogator was shouting, "Stop, stop," but we drowned him out. The guards were now hitting POWs with gun butts and the cell was in chaos.

The number five ranking officer was way back in the corner and took his time moving toward the center of the cell. (I was number seven, and not particularly anxious for him to hurry.) But just before he got to the center of the area, the cell became pin-drop quiet.

In Vietnamese, the interrogator spat out something to the guards, they grabbed number five SRO and they all left, locking the cell door behind them. The number six SRO began: "Gentlemen, the Lord's Prayer." This time we finished it.

Five courageous officers were tortured, but I think they believed it was worth it. From that Sunday on until we came home, we held a church service. We won. They lost. Forty-two men in prison pajamas followed Ned's lead. I know I will never see a better example of pure raw leadership or ever pray with a better sense of the meaning of the words.

CHAPTER 16

HANOI HILTON EXTENSION COURSES

Beyond torture, isolation, and loneliness, what made prison even harder to bear was feeling the years slip away without any sense of profit. We told each other that if we had a set of encyclopedias we could earn a PhD. Or if we had pencil and paper we could write deathless prose or poetry. Our peers in the free world were flying and fighting; we were running in place. We were missing a hundred holidays, birthdays, anniversaries; we weren't watching our children grow up. It was 1972, but we were stuck in 1967. If we ever got out we'd be a bunch of Rip Van Winkles!

But when you are locked in a cell with 20 or 30 people with good educations, you are living with knowledge. Once we were in the big cells, it took about a month to settle into a routine in which torture was the exception rather than the norm; in which talking aloud was permitted and no subjects were forbidden. We started thinking about self-improvement.

Our common POW thread was aviation: Mostly we were fighter pilots, but also navigators, electronic warfare officers, and weapon system officers. Beyond having a love for flying, we were diverse: from all states, at all ages (between 25 and 45); of all races and religions. Our ranks varied from first lieutenant and ensign to full colonel.

When President Johnson stopped the bombing in 1968, there were, as far as we were able to determine, 350 of us in the prison system. Of those, about two-thirds were Air Force and about one-third Navy—with five Marine aviators. There were also three enlisted men from helicopters shot down near the DMZ and one

Navy seaman who fell from his ship in the Gulf of Tonkin and was picked up by the enemy.

The three Air Force enlisted men, Neil Black, Art Cormier, and Bill Robinson, were on helicopters shot down in 1965. They had been tortured just like the officer pilots and kept the faith. The idea to commission them as second lieutenants was hatched. The enlisted men were taught leadership and military courses by the officers living with them. After our release in 1973, the promotion for all three was upheld, with President Nixon giving the final okay to their commissions. Commissioning those deserving enlisted men was a wonderful idea and universally supported by all the POWs.

After settling down into the new routine of life in the big cells, we discussed holding classes. The subjects would be decided by three factors: who knew something well enough to teach it; whether there was interest from other POWs in learning the subject; and whether the material could realistically be taught without pencil and paper. An overriding concern was whether the Vietnamese would allow us to gather in groups within the cell. Someone came up with the excellent idea of appointing a "school mom" (education officer) who would talk to the camp authorities. The pitch would be that we would like to share each other's knowledge by holding classes. The school mom would invite the camp authorities to sit in and learn with us. This would take away the threat of a "crowd." The school mom tactic worked, and we started to design a curriculum.

We began by asking who majored in what discipline in college or at the academies. Once we learned who had taken Spanish, for example, we got them together, and they figured out who remembered the most. We all agreed that if there was a Spanish class, all who knew some Spanish would contribute to the POW designated as the teacher.

We discovered we had a music major. He was exuberant at the idea of teaching a bunch of yank-and-bank fighter pilots some real culture. There were also two math majors in our cell. They were hesitant to try teaching math without pencils and paper. But it is easy to make a rudimentary pen from small bamboo pieces, and there were always small pieces of broken red roof tile in the bath area. We experimented (out of the sight of the guards) with grinding little bits of tile back into a powder and adding drops of water. The ink was faint but readable on the coarsest squares of toilet paper, which we hid in the middle of our little stack away from the eyes of guards who might think it some kind of cryptic information about an escape attempt.

We had courses in math, Spanish, German, Russian, English grammar, psychology, real estate, and bridge. It was a rugged marketplace of ideas. A POW might be sitting in on a math class and hear something more interesting that the German teacher was saying a few feet away. Soon the German class was larger by one and the math class smaller.

Mike Christian and I were the Spanish students. Neither of us had taken a language class before, and we discovered we didn't know tense, mood, or conjugation rules. Our "teacher" was a bit disappointed that we had to first learn grammar before we could study Spanish, but then what else did we have to do? Mike and I enjoyed the language and frequently sat in the corner of the cell practicing. Unfortunately the vocabulary of those who had studied Spanish years ago was woefully limited. When we needed a word our "teachers" didn't know—cement slab, for example—we made one up.

Mike and I were "talking Spanish" in our favorite corner one day, for instance, and needed a word for the feces barrel under the squat slab. Mike hollered to Jim, the Spanish expert. "What's the word for the crap barrel, Jim?" Jim thought a bit, and said, "shit-a-re-a." From that day on, it was *shitarea*.

Mike and I shared our toilet paper vocabulary list. Later we sat with the Spanish experts and reviewed what we'd written down. It turned out that 40 percent were real Spanish words and 60 percent were made up. Mike and I got good enough to actually carry on a decent conversation in "Spanish" with each other. But when we came home a couple of years later, there was not one Spanish-speaking person in the entire world who had any idea what we were saying.

Ted Ballard taught two unique courses: memory and hypnosis.

He was a good teacher. In the hard times, Ted used self-hypnosis to lower or eliminate pain. In the early years, I was in tap code range of Ted and tried the technique he explained to me. With a lot of practice, I became a somewhat successful self-hypnotizer. I could not use self-hypnosis for extreme pain, but it helped me through the short-term troubles like forced kneeing or a toothache.

CHAPTER 17

THE HOME FRONT

As I've said, the rescue attempt at Son Tay in November 1970 failed to free us but was a success in that it moved us from outlying camps to the big cells at the Hanoi Hilton. It was part of a general change for the better in our lives that dramatically separated the experience of the final three years in prison from the first three. The primary cause for this change was the POW families, who had taken our cause into their own hands.

When I was imprisoned in 1967, the U.S. government refused to give Gaylee the names of any other wives whose husbands were POWs. It also told her and the other families not to make an issue of the fact that their husbands, fathers, or sons were POWs: Don't talk to the press, don't do radio or TV interviews, and don't talk to service clubs. The rationale for this position was that if we became an issue, we'd be more valuable to the North Vietnamese and our release would be delayed. This was just flat wrong.

Communist delegations occasionally visited the POW camps. That was always bad. The delegations wanted to see POWs; the North Vietnamese wanted the POWs to give the "correct" answers to the delegation's predetermined questions. When a POW was taken to the delegation, all that could be seen were the POW's head, hands, and feet. The marks on the body were not visible. (POW Jeremiah Denton famously got around this when he looked straight at a camera and blinked T-O-R-T-U-R-E in Morse code.) Those POWs selected to show that we were receiving "humane and lenient treatment" were occasionally allowed to give the delegation a letter—restricted to six lines—to take home and mail directly to the POW's family. (The families were instructed by our government to slip the letter into a plastic glassine and send it to Washington for analysis by "experts" who determined that we were being tortured and, as time went by, were becoming less able to cope.) By using certain codes in those letters, we were able to sneak out names of POWs who had not been declared captured.

Growing increasingly impatient with the government's failure to help the POWs, the families decided, in effect, that enough was enough. They had to do something to help their men. In 1969, a few wives got started. Sybil Stockdale in California was one leader. Gaylee was another. Her sister and brother-in-law, Vange and Bob Renshaw, were printers. On her own, Gaylee asked Bob to print a batch of bumper stickers: "Release POWs from Hanoi." Gaylee distributed them to the few POW wives she knew. Those wives knew a handful of other wives who wanted bumper stickers too.

What started as a series of informal contacts quickly became an unofficial network of POW wives and families. With the floodgates opened, a POW organization burst upon the scene: the National League of POW/MIA Families.

Sybil was the league's first president. She was as organized and outgoing as her POW husband, Jim, was tough. How tough was Jim Stockdale? Stories about his resistance in prison are legendary, including the incident in which he smashed his face with a piece of wood and deeply cut his scalp with a broken shard of glass when he was about to be paraded before a delegation of fellow traveling foreign journalists and politicians. Sybil became so dedicated to the organization that she rented out their home in California and moved to the D.C. area so she could lobby government leaders on POW issues.

We had no idea that our families were trying to rally the American public behind us, or that the National League of POW/MIA Families had demanded that the North Vietnamese treat the American POWs according to the Geneva Convention and give a full accounting of all known POWs and KIAs (Killed in Action). We did not know that the small improvements we began to experience in our lives had been caused by our families' actions. I myself knew just one thing: It was indescribably difficult surviving the first three years of prison, and, if treatment had not improved, I would not have made it through the next three years.

Never once in all that time did I see any sign of the Red Cross. But I did begin to see evidence of the league's activism and its focus on our brutal treatment. Gradually we got to send and receive letters. The Vietnamese restricted all letters to six lines, and a letter got through only every four to six months. A rare six-line letter, however, was infinitely better than no letter. A second benefit of the pressure that POW families put on Vietnam for better treatment was that families were also allowed to send to us a 3-kilogram (6.6 pounds) package every two months.

With great love, thought, and hope, Gaylee and Dawn prepared my packages. The rules set by the Vietnamese allowed clothing, non-perishable food items, medicine, and a few pictures. According to government instructions, the package was to be sealed at the post office. Gaylee bought a special scale to make sure I would get the full 6.6 pounds. She always took a few pieces of hard candy to the post office to add if the package was even an ounce short.

Most packages never arrived in our cells. They were lost, stolen, discarded, evaporated, or whatever, in the international and Vietnamese postal systems. The packages I actually received at the prison would weigh a pound, two at the most. Generally the Vietnamese gave us the box it was shipped in; I recognized Gaylee's handwriting. But the box was always much bigger than the contents. Sometimes there were telltale signs of what had been sent and stolen—freeze-dried coffee grounds, for instance, but no coffee.

In 1970, a POW in our cell received a package with a few items the Vietnamese had not bothered to take. Among them were a half dozen or so tiny sugar packets—the kind with a one-inch square picture that you find in diners and coffee shops. The picture on the sugar packet showed Neil Armstrong stepping onto the moon.

We knew that John Kennedy had announced a plan to send a man to the moon "in this decade," but all of us were in prison well before July 11, 1969, when the event occurred. That picture filled us with excitement, joy, and pride. We had done it! Within minutes of finding the sugar packet, we were on the walls tapping out this message: "AM[erican] ON MOON." It was the best news we had since becoming POWs. Neil Armstrong, a year after he landed, made us—a pajama-clad, beat and bent, scruffy group of POWs—the proudest Americans on the planet. His accomplishment validated America, and it validated us too.

——

The Vietnamese did allow some of the pictures our families sent us to get through. Oddly, before giving them to us they encased them in loose clear plastic. We studied every detail in every picture. Each of us with children spent hours analyzing how they had changed and grown. It took me a while to recognize my daughter, Dawn, after four years. The pretty little girl I remembered had grown into a beautiful young woman (taking after her mother). Over the last couple of years in prison I received 11 pictures. I'm sure those pictures got 1,100 hours of looking. It wasn't just Dawn or Gaylee that I studied; it was every tree, couch, and detail. In one picture, Dawn was leaning on a car. I wondered if Gaylee had traded in the old Rambler station wagon. Did my brother-in-law Bob help? Each picture generated a thousand thoughts. What a blessing they were, even if they created more questions than answers.

I punched tiny holes in the corner of the plastic that covered the pictures. With thread from my blanket, I made a string of pictures and hung it below the bars on the window. It was as close to home as I could get. As more POWs received pictures, more pictures hung below the bars around the cell. While I was looking at Konnie Trautman's pictures one day, he began explaining all the details. Not long after, while Konnie was looking at my pictures, I said, "Konnie, let's swap families for a week." He thought a minute and said okay. We made the trade. When others stopped by to look at my new family, I told them all about everyone in the photos, where they lived and what they did. Konnie's slab was not far from mine. He could hear me as I described my new family; if I said something wrong he corrected me. Over time many of us swapped families. We were one large family anyhow.

Just as we shared package items with all POWs in the cell, we also shared letters. During the last three years, the average for all POWs was about two letters a year—six lines each. The best news was when a POW received a letter from home saying that they had heard that he was alive. I received such a letter about two years after I was shot down. There was no guarantee that I would live until I was released—whenever that might be. But at least my family had definite knowledge about me and knew that I wasn't dead yet.

After the guard came to the cell and gave a POW a letter, we would "give him time and space." He would find a corner of the cell, and we would all move toward the other end. We tried not to watch him, but we did. His expression was telling: happy, calm, sad, or worried. Families knew our health had deteriorated and our bodies had been tortured. It was obvious in most letters that they had chosen their words carefully. In the main, the six lines were newsy, rather than intimate, seeking to avoid writing anything that would add stress to our situation.

After a POW had read his letter several times and pondered everything in it, then it was our turn. The POW would stand in the middle of the cell, as we huddled around him, and begin to read, "Dear Wayne ..." Right away we interrupted him, "Who is the letter from, who signed it?" "My wife, Betty," he'd reply. Of course we all knew Betty; her picture was on his string.

Each item in the letter generated conversation. A reader rarely got through all six lines without interruptions. News of someone else's family was just about as good as news from our own families. Letters were major events.

Ray was a tough POW who'd grown up on a farm in the middle of America. He had been captured in Laos, and very few Americans captured there survived until being turned over to the North Vietnamese. He'd gone four years without word from home when he finally received a letter. If ever a man deserved a good letter, it was Ray.

It began with the usual routine: the guard appearing in the cell with a letter. Who would it go to? Finally it was Ray's turn. We were all happy for him. He went to a back corner, and we sauntered to the front part, made small talk, and sneaked peeks at him. He sat there longer than normal. It was obvious he had reread the letter several times. Between the re-reads, his face was blank. After much too long a time, I said, "Okay, Ray, it's our turn." Ray slowly looked around and said without expression, "Sorry, this is not a good letter to share."

Everyone shared their letters—we would have no part of him keeping it to himself. We began to badger him: "Come on, Ray; we all share." "It's our turn—we need the news." Ray finally said, "No, it is not good news, it is only for me." The more he resisted, the more we insisted. He finally relented. He walked to the middle of the cell, and, as we gathered close, he began to read.

"Dear Raymond," he hesitated and looked up, but none of us said a word. From what he had said before, and how he looked now, we knew better than to interrupt this one.

If the following is not the exact wording of the letter, it is very close:

> Dear Raymond, this has been a bad year. Hail took our crops—no insurance. Your brother-in-law borrowed your speedboat, hit a rock, it sank. Aunt Clarice died suddenly last August. Dad tipped the tractor but only broke his leg. Your 4-H heifer grew up, became a cow, but she died calving—calf too. We think of you often. Mom and Dad.

There was dead silence for perhaps a minute. Finally someone said, "Ray, read it again, maybe there's a hidden meaning." He shook his head. After more encouragement, he read it again. When he got to the part "your speedboat sank," a POW in the back could no longer hold in his muffled laugh. When Ray read, "she died calving," the snickers had turned into open, uncontrolled laughter.

In six years of prison, there was never more genuine slap-your-thighs, roll-on-your-side laughter. We were in stitches and couldn't stop. Ray, bless him, realized how ridiculous, how totally inappropriate it was for a family to write that letter to someone in prison. He joined in the hilarity.

We were only allowed to keep the letters for a short time before the Vietnamese took them back "for safe keeping." While Ray had that letter in the cell, every day someone would get it and read it aloud, causing us all to break up again. From then on, every time the guard came with a letter, we each hoped it was ours—but if it wasn't, we all hoped it would be another letter for Ray.

CHAPTER 18

PRISON TALK

What do 25 adult men talk about when locked in a cell for years on end? Everything.

Sometimes in the big cells the discussions got heated. In one cell, they came up with a rule to prevent things from turning nasty. If a POW wanted to express an opinion without rebuttal or further discussion, he began by saying, "This is an IDV." (IDV stood for "individual declaration of view.") Then he had his say and that was that. If he wanted a debate or discussion, which was the case most of the time, he omitted the acronym.

But while all things came within our purview, most of our talk centered on women and wives. We all talked about how we met our spouses and what about them we missed most. Sooner or later the talk came down to the nitty gritty: had they been faithful and would they be there when we got home?

Most POWs began by telling their cellmates how they met their wives. Ned Shuman, who, as I've described, was one of our leaders, had one of the best marriage stories. When we were in the big cells, it was a certainty that every so often someone would say, "Ned, tell us again how you married Sue."

"I've already told it several times," he'd reply.

But we'd point out that someone new had just come into the cell and hadn't heard it yet and continue to badger Ned until he gave in. He actually enjoyed telling the story and added details every time.

The essence of it was that on a three-day weekend before the war, Ned—then a young Naval aviator—had driven from Virginia to South Carolina to be the best man at a friend's wedding. After the wedding, he had somehow hooked up with Sue, one of the bridesmaids. Forty-eight hours later, he awoke with a bad hangover in bed with Sue, who was now his new wife. The marriage tried to find a reason for being after the fact and never succeeded.

By the time Ned finished with side stories about the mother-in-law from hell, etc., we were all in stitches, even those of us who'd heard all this before. Ned was dubious that Sue would be there when he got home. She was, but not for long.

Chuck Tyler's wife was a good-looking, leggy young woman pictured in the miniest of miniskirts. Hers was a very popular photograph in the cell. Chuck talked wistfully about how she was a "free spirit." He said more than once, "I wouldn't be surprised if a divorce happened soon after we get home." It did.

Darrel Pyle had not been married long to Nancy before he was shot down. His stories about her were the best of all the wife stories. Nancy was a gourmet cook—any kind of food. Anything he killed or caught, she cleaned and cooked. Her social skills were outstanding. She was beautiful and the greatest sex partner any pilot had ever had.

After all the public relations work Darrel was doing, John Borling, Darrel's long-time cellmate and friend, started feeling insecure about his own wife. He began making up stories about her virtues so that she would be competitive, but he could never quite make her equal to Darrel's Nancy. At the beginning of Darrel's first call to his perfect wife after we were released, she said, "I want a divorce."

There was a high rate of failure among POW marriages, but surprisingly little rancor. We'd had time to understand in advance what the wives faced, living in a society that had suddenly and almost hysterically embraced immediate gratification of desire. Many wives waited a year, two years, three. But there was no end in sight. Some needed a companion; some simply fell out of love when there was no one there to love. Renunciation of temptation was not part of the temper of the times.

When we came home we were different people and so were our wives, with the six or so years of different experiences standing like a barrier between us. I think many couples tried to make a go of it without acknowledging that at some level they were now strangers who only had in common the fact that they had once known each other well. I was lucky. Gaylee and I picked up where we left off, agreeing to treat the absence as a hiccup in our relationship. Unlike many other POWs and their wives, we didn't dwell on what had happened to us or try to deeply analyze it. We were lucky because we stayed very busy. I jumped into a political race soon after getting home, and Gaylee was a sort of co-candidate. We were so involved with people, schedules, media, and stump speeches that we didn't have time to "adjust." The only thing Gaylee asked of me was that I stop sending unconscious messages in my sleep by using the tap code on her body.

But there were domestic successes as well as domestic failures. I remember Dick Bolstad, who was in a big cell with me in 1971, listening wistfully as I talked about Gaylee and the other men talked about their wives. He hadn't had time to marry his fiancée, Sissy, before shipping out. But he was as enthusiastic as any of us, telling how beautiful Sissy was inside and out, and how he was sure she would be there when we got home. We didn't say so to Dick, but we thought that if she were the fantastic woman he claimed she was, she'd meet someone else while he was cooling his heels in prison year after year, especially without a wedding ring to anchor her down.

When Dick finally got a package, among the remnants left after the camp commander and guards had pillaged it, were a couple of photographs. Sissy really was a beautiful woman. Now we old married guys really began to rib Dick, enumerating all the reasons why someone who looked like that, and wasn't already legally bound, wouldn't wait for a guy like him.

But Dick turned out to be right. Sissy was there when he came home. They got married and had a beautiful little girl. When Gaylee and I have visited them, we have been struck by how happy they are.

We squeezed in a few other subjects besides women. Several POWs, for instance, had great recall of books and a way with words to tell the stories in detail and interestingly. Among the great book reporters were Jack Van Loan, John Borling, Barry Bridger, and Jim Young. Bill Metzger, who was in a four-person cell with Jim Young, told me not long ago that Jim retold all 11 of the Horatio Hornblower books by C.S. Forester.

A few of the favorite movies that we told over and over again were *Dr. Zhivago*, *The Great Gatsby*, and *Sand Pebbles*. Some of the outstanding movie tellers were Jim Bettinger, Chuck Zuhowski, John McCain, and Chuck Rice. One of the three POWs in a cell with Chuck later told me that Chuck "told" a different movie every night for three weeks. Bill said, "Leo, I swear Chuck must have lived in a movie house before he got shot down—it was great."

Not all movies or books had to be real. Jim Warner, a creative young Marine aviator, was an exceptionally talented teller of movies that had never been made. Jim could create the theme, story, and characters, and describe the visual camera shots—all out of whole cloth. His were some of the very best movies that we "saw" at the Hanoi Hilton.

We also had top ten lists. Long before there was David Letterman, there was Mike Christian, the guy with whom I practiced Spanish with a majority of made-up words. Mike was a handsome Naval officer who was tough as they came. If he was forced to give an inch to the Vietnamese, the next day he took back two.

I lived with Mike for a year toward the end of our six years in Hanoi. We were in big cells with about 25 POWs. With that many men, there were more topics to talk about, more discussions and debates to have, and more classes to take. But boredom was still an enemy lying in wait for us. It was Mike Christian who had a new idea, which immediately caught on with all POWs, when he said one day, "Leo, you know the first ten items of clothing I'm going to buy when we get home?" Mike had memorized them in priority order and immediately rattled them off. Then he asked me, "Do you know the first ten people I'm going to call when I get home?" He rattled them off as well. Then he told me a couple of other lists he had thought through. One of them involved the top ten people he would never talk to even if he ran into them face to face. Jane Fonda was at the top of that list.

Soon list mania infected everyone in the cell—then expanded to other cells. We developed lists for the first ten things we would eat, the first ten trips we would take, the top ten cities we would visit, the top ten cars we wanted. I reviewed them each day so I would not forget. Of course we started comparing lists and plagiarizing shamelessly.

———

We had a discussion one day about the speeches we would give if we were ever released and if anyone back home was interested enough to listen. Bob Lilly suggested we should do a Toastmasters class in the cell. In college he had been on the debate team and later had taken a Toastmasters course.

Bob said, "We will need a speech timer—who volunteers?"

Chuck volunteered.

"What's your pulse rate?" Bob asked.

"It varies a lot."

"You won't do. We need someone with a steady pulse and best if it is about 60 beats per minute."

John Stavast spoke up, "I already know how to speak, and so I'm not interested in any Toastmasters stuff, but I have a good heart, pulse about 60." He became the official counter.

Rather than just asking us as a group, Bob individually asked each POW to sign up for his course. He gave a little pitch about how Toastmasters would help us better explain our experiences to the organizations he confidently predicted would be interested in hearing about them. A high percentage of us signed up.

Time came for the first Toastmasters class, and 14 of the 25 POWs in the cell showed up. ("Showing up" meant we sat on our bed boards in one end of the cell.) It was obvious that the other nine, however much they pretended to be doing something else, were listening to see how things would go.

Bob had given a lot of thought to his class. "Gentlemen, no matter how well you speak in public now, this class will make you better," he began. "So listen up; here are the expected results if you stick with the syllabus."

Several of us glanced around making eye contact with one another thinking, "Whoa, what have we gotten ourselves into?"

Bob spelled out what we'd gain:

- Be comfortable giving impromptu speeches.
- Develop and present ideas.
- Control nervousness when speaking to a group.
- Learn gestures and body movement as part of speaking.
- Learn how to appeal to the self-interest of the audience.

There may have been a couple of other goals, but at this point the other nine POWs had stopped talking, started listening, and moved closer. None of us knew this Bob. Until now, we had all been through the same hell and were more or less equals in a prisoner-of-war camp. Suddenly Bob had become a teacher.

Bob reconfirmed with John that he was going to time the speeches. Next he asked for a volunteer to count the "ahs" in each speech. By now, I was a bit anxious as we were randomly assigned to speak from three to five minutes, and so I volunteered to count the "ahs." John used his 60 heartbeats per minute for time, and we began. The speeches ranged from mediocre to polished. The two-week class added more students than it dropped and everyone "graduated." To his credit, when we came home Bob contacted Toastmasters International and told the story about having a Toastmasters class in the Hanoi Hilton. The organization found it such an interesting story that they recognized us retroactively as a club and sanctioned the graduates as having successfully fulfilled the real class credits while in prison.

––––––

If 24 POWs were in a cell, there were often ten or so separate conversations going on. The subjects were the same—when will the war end, how are the wife and kids doing, sports, and fishing. There were rarely stories that had not been heard before.

Listening to them day after day, I determined to find a new topic of interest that would draw out my cellmates. I started a casual conversation with Bill, a POW from Wisconsin. "Why do you think that folks raised like us in the Midwest have higher values— you know, more honesty and that sort of thing—than those from the East or West coasts?"

"Because our parents had better values," Bill answered.

"Why is that?"

"Because they worked hard and lived off the soil."

"That's exactly right," Norlan, a POW from Iowa, chipped in. "My parents were farmers and worked harder than the big city slickers on the coasts."

Ray, an Ivy Leaguer from Connecticut, hearing these comments, couldn't restrain himself. "That's a bunch of bullshit."

Soon everyone in the cell was involved in the argument, which became heated and lasted over two hours. After the first five minutes, I pulled back and lay down on my bedboard to listen. It was a great afternoon.

A few days later, I got another one going about why Air Force pilots had fewer accidents than Navy pilots, throwing out a made-up accident rate for Navy men and theorizing that it was because we Air Force men were better trained. In the rhetorical melee that followed, the Naval aviators never questioned the premise but argued hard on the causes. Again I pulled out just after things got hot and enjoyed another good day while lying on my bedboard.

It took a couple of months and several more heated discussions before my cellmates finally caught on to what I was up to. They all gave me a bad time. These discussions took place the last months of 1972, our last Christmas in prison. We drew names for pretend presents. In addition to having my name in the hat, I also got a special gift from everybody. It was a large pebble they sneaked into the cell. The toilet paper wrapping had this inscription. "To the Harmony Officer, Leo. Let he who is without sin cast the first stone."

MIKE'S FLAG

Though things got marginally better for us after 1970, we never forgot who or where we were. We all knew that we were marked forever and would always see things—particularly things involving our country—from a different angle of vision than that of our fellow citizens.

When I finally came home, I got involved in politics, eventually serving in the Washington state senate from 1988 to 1992. It was a time of heated debates about desecrating the United States flag. The Washington legislature had scheduled its own debate, and our caucus asked me to speak in favor of protecting the flag. I agreed to do it. I had been in the senate for two years and never yet mentioned my POW experience on the senate floor.

Generally when a senator spoke, the initial polite attention was gradually overwhelmed by side conversations among the legislators. On this afternoon, a flag resolution was introduced with the usual reading and paper shuffling, and I stood up, the first to speak. I glanced at the gallery, normally sparsely occupied by a handful of spectators but on this day full. The room was silent. My seat was near the rear, the normal location for freshman senators. I took a deep breath, glanced at my speech outline on my desktop, and looked at the members as I took up the microphone. To my surprise, all the senators had turned in their chairs to face me.

My speech was short—only about three minutes—and, unknown to me, a concerned citizen in the gallery was taking notes, and, a few months later, a summary of my speech appeared in *Reader's Digest*.

I spoke that day about Mike Christian and something he had done in 1972, our last year in prison. By that time, we were allowed outside most days for a few minutes to pour a bucket of water over ourselves from a concrete tank in the prison yard and call it a bath. A gutter ran by the tank, under the prison wall and into the Hanoi drainage system. While 25 naked POWs poured water over themselves, there was always a bit of milling around that delayed the guards locking us back up.

During one of these moments, Mike saw a slimy rag in the gutter and whispered to me, "Leo, there's something in the gutter I want to get back to the cell—keep the guard's attention." As a prisoner, you scrounge anything you can and help others to do the same. In this case I helped by talking loudly to draw attention while Mike stooped over and hid the rag in his pajama top. Mission accomplished. Back inside the cell we saw that it was a small handkerchief. Soap was precious but when Mike asked us we all chipped in a little to clean the cloth. Tattered gray was as good as he could get it.

Mike scrounged a small piece of red roof tile and laboriously ground it into a powder, which, mixed with a bit of water, became a faded red or maroon color to make the flag's stripes. We had gotten a bit of medicine in the last year of our captivity, usually a blue pill of unknown provenance prescribed for all afflictions. Mike patiently leached the color out of one of the pills and used it to make a blue square in the upper left of the handkerchief. With a needle made from bamboo wood and thread pulled from our single blanket, he stitched little white stars on this field of blue.

It took Mike a couple of weeks to make the flag—working at night under his mosquito net so the guards couldn't see him. Early one morning, he got up before the guards were active and held up the flag, waving it as if in a breeze. He said in a loud whisper, "Look here, gang." As we turned Mike's way, we automatically came to attention and saluted. Some of us began to cry.

Mike knew—we all knew—the Vietnamese would eventually find the flag during one of their periodic inspections when they stripped us naked and ran us outside so they could go through our belongings.

The night after they found the flag they took Mike to the torture cell and beat him badly. Sometime after midnight they pushed him back into our cell. He was bloody and semi-conscious, so badly hurt that even his voice was gone.

But as I've said, Mike was a tough man. He recovered in a couple of weeks and immediately started looking for another piece of cloth.

CHAPTER 20

CHRISTMAS 1972

The end of 1972 was an intense time. We were able to follow the presidential election because the North Vietnamese were convinced that Senator George McGovern would win and filled camp radio with daily news booming his antiwar candidacy. During the campaign, the North Vietnamese often quoted McGovern. One of his quotes stuck in our craw: "If elected president I will go to Vietnam and beg on my knees for the release of our POWs." Every POW was instantly enraged. During torture, many of us had been forced to "stand" on our knees until we passed out. To picture an American president offering to kneel to those who had done this to us was an abomination. We held our own presidential vote. Of the 189 POWs available to communicate by tap code, the vote was 188 for Nixon and one for McGovern. We never found out who the one was.

In addition to McGovern's overwhelming defeat, other good signs began appearing in the fall of 1972. We received a little medicine; torture abated; we got to stay outside the cells for longer periods at bath time. In addition to our two meals a day and two dishes per meal—soup (cabbage, pumpkin, or green) and bread or rice—occasionally a third dish appeared. It was about a third of a cup of raw sugar.

We were always looking for omens and naturally we wondered why they were giving us sugar. The answer that we liked best was that sugar contains calories. Thanks to our families, the North Vietnamese had begun receiving bad publicity for their brutalization of us POWs. If we were to be released in the near future, our death camp appearance would validate this charge. So maybe the sugar meant they were fattening us up for release.

Hanoi was hot in summer, cold in winter. In summer the old cellblocks soaked up the heat during the day and radiated it at night. Winter temperatures would get down to 45 degrees. That's not cold in Minnesota where I grew up, but without heat, and sleeping on concrete with a worn blanket, 45 degrees is freezing. As part of improved treatment during the last "big cell" years, we received a pair of green, ankle-length cotton socks. They were not Eddie Bauer, but they were a lot better than no socks at all and cut the chill.

When Christmas had come during those first brutal POW years, it was just another day. We, of course, had no presents, no trees, and no church service to attend. We knew it was Christmas and mentally tried to celebrate the miraculous birth. Once we were in the big cells, we could at least exchange family Christmas stories.

On Christmas 1972 we decided to have a Christmas tree made out of our green socks. Mike Christian came up with the idea and suggested it to the SRO. The SRO thought at least a minute and said, "Let's see if we can get away with it." We needed rice paste made from steamed rice mixed with a tad of water and squeezed into stickiness. Mike had tested its powers of adherence with one of his socks. He put rice paste on one side of it and pressed it against the wall. After he held it in place a few minutes, it stuck. By experimenting, he found the right consistency of the paste—not too wet, not too dry.

Fortunately, it was unusually mild and we could do without our green socks. Mike collected them and laid them out on his bed slab. He decided to start on the bottom with a double row of six socks, three on each side pointing slightly up like pine tree branches. Above that were two rows of four socks, two rows of two, then one sock pointing straight up at the top center. A 25-sock Christmas tree.

Luckily we got rice on December 24. We saved plenty and started making paste in the afternoon. Mike was diligent, critically checking the viscosity. With toilet paper he made a template on the wall. We dabbed the paste on the socks and stuck them up. Every-one got into it. We were kids again decorating the tree at home.

When Mike stuck the last sock straight up on top, Jim Seahorn suggested a star. It wasn't long before Jack, the resident artist, had a small star fashioned from toilet paper. There was our tree, star and all. We all stood back and admired it. The tree was the conversation topic all day. In the prisoner-of-war camp setting, the green-sock Christmas tree brought home the true meaning of Christmas. We had been through years of torture and tough times and through it all we supported and depended on each other. Now, in better times and hints that this hell might be ending, we were celebrating the Lord's birth with our brothers. Most of us still remember this as one of the most memorable Christmases in our lives.

The guards saw the tree on Christmas morning and acted like it wasn't there. That was our signal we could make it better. We made various Christmas tree ornaments from toilet paper. Then we had a Christmas gift drawing. Once we each had a name, we created gift cards. The blue pills made decent ink, and we put each name on the card and what the gift was. We promised that when we got home we would send the real gifts. We did.

———

But the real reason Christmas was special that year had to do with something that began a week before the holiday on the evening of December 18.

Occasionally during our years in Hanoi, we sometimes heard a "recce" (reconnaissance plane, F-4 Phantom usually) taking photos blast low over Hanoi at or near supersonic. Generally we would hear flak firing at it. But, on December 18, the sound was different—a muffled sound, at first barely audible, and then slowly building. I will never forget the look on each POW's face as we realized what it was. We had often speculated and hoped that Nixon might bring the war to North Vietnam—right into Hanoi—using full airpower. Was this finally it, a month after his reelection and a week before Christmas? Yes!

The roar overhead grew ever louder. Intermingled with the jet sounds, we heard SAM after SAM blasting off their launch pads. The constant flak sound came from every direction; small arms fire came from the prison area. Beside the heavy B-52 noise, occasionally fighters zipped through—some were Wild Weasels, my old plane, trying to negate the SAMs; some were MiGs going after the B-52s. Next the muffled sound of bombs began. At first far off, then closer, and then on top of us. We knew each bomber carried 72 500-pound bombs. The explosions rippled in continuous waves. We felt certain that the B-52 crews knew from the recce flights exactly where we were and that they were allowed to bomb within 2,000 feet of our camps. (Dropping from some 30,000 feet there was not much room for error.) Plaster fell from the ceilings; the dim lights flickered on and off a few times and then went off for the rest of the night. The large windows high up in our cells were not bricked shut, and we had a view of a patch of sky. We could see the show: bomb explosions, tracers, and periodically the rocket flame of a SAM.

As if talking to the B-52 crews, we shouted: "Get the bastards" and "Finally!" and "The war is over!" Someone yelled, "Remember Uncle Ho's cabin." (Supposedly Ho Chi Minh had a mountain cabin off-limits to American bombing.)

We were in the middle of it but had no fear. Bud Day summed up everyone's feeling. "If a B-52 is hit and its string of bombs dumps directly on us, it's over." He continued, "If we survive the bombing, the Vietnamese will sign the accords, and it'll be over." He ended, "Either way, it's over."

The bombing lasted 15 minutes or more. Later in the night, a second wave of B-52s arrived, then a third. Finally the sky was quiet. We all talked at once. Would this force the Vietnamese to sign the peace accords the camp radio had talked about for months? Would the B-52s come in again? How would the guards and camp authorities treat us tomorrow morning?

Sleep was short that night as bunkmates speculated in whispers. The guards arrived later than usual the next morning, heightening our speculation that the camp authorities would make us pay for the raids. But when the cell door opened, there were no beatings and only one word: "Bath." We took our time at the tank and were not hurried back in. As the prison routine continued throughout the day, rather than animosity from the guard, there seemed to be a feeling of calm. As we discussed events in the cell, we came to the conclusion the Vietnamese too realized that the war would soon be over. They realized that having been reelected, President Nixon did not have to worry about another term and would pull out all the stops. The Vietnamese knew that if they began to brutalize us again, their allies in the "international community" would not be able to protect them from American wrath.

The next night we heard once again the low rumble of jet engines in the distance. Again the SAMs, flak, small-arms fire, and fighters. There were a couple of very loud airborne explosions. Sadly we knew it was a B-52 taking a SAM, and the plane exploding with all the men still on board.

The night of December 20 was the same routine, although even more SAMs were launched, leading us to speculate that if the bombing continued much longer, they would soon run out of SAMs. (Before the U.S. bombing campaign was over they did.) At one point, our window's patch of sky lit up in a brilliant and horrifying explosion as a B-52 took a direct SAM hit right in front of us. About 25 seconds later we felt and heard the explosion.

The Christmas Bombing was officially Operation Linebacker II. It started on December 18 and ended December 29—continuing every night except Christmas. The U.S. flew 3,000 sorties and dropped 40,000 tons of bombs. Fifteen B-52s were lost along with 11 other American aircraft. Linebacker II unblocked the peace talks stalled the previous October and pushed the North Vietnamese back to the table on January 8, 1973. Thirty days after the final bomb, on January 27, 1973, Henry Kissinger and Le Duc Tho signed the Paris Peace Accords. They required that all prisoners of all combat nations be told within ten days that the war was over.

During our years in Hanoi, we got pretty good at figuring out why the North Vietnamese did certain things certain ways. But at some level, we never really fathomed them. For example, why did they send most of my wife's letters back to her stamped "Deceased" when she knew I had been captured alive? And why, after they signed the peace accords ending the war, did they keep lying to us? On the morning of the tenth day after the accords were signed, they made the announcement over the camp radio: "There has been no progress in peace talks, the perfidious Americans will not negotiate reasonably." (The Vietnamese found a few big words, like perfidious, and used them over and over in their broadcasts.)

But then, late that afternoon, the guards opened several cell doors and told us to go outside. For the first time, POWs from several cells stood together. The camp commander walked toward the end of the group, a guard put down a little box and the commander climbed on. The prison yard was pin-drop quiet. The commander simply said, "The war is over. You blackest criminals [a favorite term for us] will be released in four groups 15 days apart." With no expression, he continued, "The longest-held criminals will go first."

That was it. We were sent back into our cells. Rather than cheering, back slapping, or jumping—there was silence. I had an apple-sized lump in my throat and tears ran down my cheeks. There were not many dry eyes that afternoon.

CHAPTER 21

LEAVING HELL

The last week of February 1973 the first group of POWs was issued civilian clothes and put on a bus headed to Hanoi's Gia Lam airport for the trip home. The three-fourths of us who remained in prison had no way to be sure if they were really going home. It could still be a trick.

I was sick and running a high temperature with chills. They put me in solitary—ostensibly so others would not catch whatever I had. On March 4, I saw others of the "vintage" POWs getting clothes. My heart sank. That was my group. Wasn't I going home, too? An hour later a guard brought clothes for me. I joined the others, including my backseater, Harry. It was the first time we were together in six years. We hugged and searched for words. I had known that he was alive because of the tap code, but finally talking to him again was liberation in itself.

We were loaded on the bus, driven through Hanoi, and taken to a small hangar at Gia Lam airport. As we drove past the tarmac, we saw no American aircraft. The hangar was empty except for our guards and two older Vietnamese men, standing by a table. Again we wondered if it was a trick. But soon we heard the sound of an engine. We looked up and saw a USAF C-141 in the traffic pattern.

A few minutes later we were taken to an area across the tarmac where a crowd gathered. After some chatter between the guards and a high-ranking North Vietnamese officer, we were told to get off the bus and form two lines. We were called off by name, according to our shoot down date.

The C-141 was parked 200 yards to the right and 50 yards straight ahead was a table. Behind the table sat a Vietnamese officer and a United States Air Force colonel. When our name was called we marched forward, stopped in front of the table, and saluted the colonel. He returned the salute and put a check by our name on his POW list. An Air Force enlisted man took us by the arm and escorted us to the tail ramp of the C-141. At the bottom of the ramp, the escort went back to get another POW, and the best-looking nurses in the entire world (and also the first women we had seen in six years) took us into the plane.

Those shot down on the same date went alphabetically. This meant that Harry, who had been 42 inches behind me for 92.5 missions, now went ahead. He looked back at me and winked as he went up the ramp.

We were buckled up, handed a cold beer, and given copies of current magazines, as the C-141's engines started. I was in a litter, but my spirits were higher than my temperature. There was subdued POW chatter until the aircraft taxied, turned onto the active runway, added power, and broke ground. *That* was the instant. Six years of POW emotion spontaneously exploded. We were leaving hell.

———

The three-hour flight from Hanoi to Clark Air Base in the Philippines could have been 30 minutes or 30 hours. Several of the C-141's crew members told us we were viewed as heroes and would be welcomed home with open arms. We were not so sure. All of us who had survived the horrible torture of the past few years had gone past giving out just our name, rank, serial number, and date of birth. Would we be welcomed the first week and court-martialed the second week? Would we be allowed to stay in the military?

Our doubts were answered as the plane came to a stop on the Clark Air Base tarmac. We looked out the windows and saw hundreds of Air Force men in uniform and their wives and kids. Everyone, it seemed, had little American flags. Dignitaries were arriving; a red carpet was being rolled out. While we waited for the staircase to get in place, the door was opened, and we got a better look at the military families there to greet us. Harry looked at them and said, "Jeez, they're fat."

Over the years in prison, I had learned how to walk fairly well with two destroyed knees and a back broken more than once during torture. We had been told television crews would be filming our exit from the plane. One of those good-looking nurses insisted that she would help me down the stairs. I insisted harder that she would not. I knew Gaylee, Dawn, and other family members would be watching. I wanted my visual message to them to be that I was okay. They had worried about me for six years; it was enough.

As each of us exited the door, a loud cheer went up. We stopped at the bottom, saluted the ranking general, shook hands with the other officers in line, and boarded the bus. A short ride and we were at the hospital. The American kids attending the Clark Air Base elementary school had worked hard. Every hospital hallway had dozens of welcome home crayon pictures.

Three of us were assigned to a room. The floors were shiny and clean; the walls were painted white and adorned with pictures. The windows had glass and went up and down; we had forgotten about that. And oh, those beds—mattresses, pillows, and perfectly white sheets tucked in smartly at the edges. I opened the door on the side of the room. There it was—round, white glistening porcelain with a donut lid and cover: a toilet. I pushed down on the handle and the water left with that beautiful gushing sound. It was addictive— I flushed it again, again, and again. Jack Bomar grabbed me by the scruff of the neck, pulled me out, and took his turn flushing ... again and again.

———

Next came what I had thought about for six years. In 1973 there were still operators in the phone system. Our families were briefed that if they were on the telephone and a call came from "their" POW, the operator would break into the call and hook us up. There were limited overseas lines so we had to hold our first call to ten minutes. After that, whenever a line was available, we could talk and talk.

I had thought for six years what my first words to Gaylee would be. When my turn came, I was ready. The operator said, "Just a moment, sir," I rehearsed my words again. As the phone rang, my heart pounded, and I swallowed hard. Her beautiful voice hadn't changed, "Leo, is that you?" I stuck with my plan. "Gaylee, I would have called sooner but I've been all tied up."

We had so many questions; so many things to say to start our six-year catch-up. We struggled. It was a massive mountain, and we couldn't find the path to start climbing it. That first phone call was difficult, but, on the second call later that day, the dam broke and words flooded out. Our love, our bond, our family would soon be together after so many difficult years.

———

After the phone calls, it was into the doctor's office for a cursory check—full medical needs would be met later at the major military hospitals in the States. I was still running a high fever. Initial diagnosis was it was some form of malaria. The doctor ran a couple of tests and decided it was not infectious. "If you can walk, you can go," he said. I told him I could have been the walking dead and still would have made it onto the plane.

The mess hall had never served all three meals at 3 p.m. But on this day they served us everything except green weed soup and dirty steamed rice. We had breakfast, lunch, and dinner at the same time. The doctors warned us not to overeat but acknowledged, correctly, that we probably would.

We were issued our new uniforms, given a cash advance, and taken back to our hospital room for a rest. We were just settling in for a snooze when an echoing sound filled the hallway. Although it was six years since we had heard that sound, there was no mistaking it. It was a woman in high heels. Our POW hospital wing had rooms on each side of a long hallway. As if on command, POW heads popped out of every room. No one was disappointed. When we left the States in the mid-1960s, adult clothing was still conservative. The miniskirt, a fad we had missed, was still happening in the Philippines. Down the hospital hallway came a beautiful young Philippine woman whose skirt was *maybe* 12 inches long. Every

POW head turned to follow her body from one end of the hallway to the corner at the other end.

They opened the PX just for POWs at 6 p.m. I bought nice pieces of jewelry for Gaylee and Dawn and then something for myself. I've always been time conscious, and it had been a hardship to live six years without a watch. I asked, "What color watches— silver or gold—are in fashion nowadays?" The saleslady judiciously replied, "Well sir, that depends on what you wear." I bought one of each.

Day two at Clark Air Base was the start of the debriefing that would be concluded back in the States. Day three began the long trip to Hawaii. Our flight plan was to stop in Honolulu, where we would then separate, with Air Force and Navy POWs going off to the major Air Force and Navy hospitals nearest their homes. I was for Scott Air Force Base, just outside of St. Louis. With tailwinds, the 5,280 miles from the Philippines to Hickam Air Force Base was eight to nine hours.

Still running a fever, I was in a litter in the back of the plane. It's hard to tell if your temperature is high just by touching your own forehead. But when your thoughts start getting fuzzy, you know it is really getting up there. When I left Clark, it was just over 100. A couple of hours out: 102. Five hours into the flight—I knew the time because I had a silver watch on my left wrist and a gold one on the right—it was 103 degrees. We were still a couple of hours from Hawaii, and my thoughts were no longer orderly. I had a hard time reading the thermometer, but it looked to be over 104 degrees. I motioned to the nurse and said, "This close to home, I'm not going to expire now!"

"We'll make sure you don't," she replied, but the words seemed to lack confidence. Thinking as clearly as I could, I asked them to pack me with ice, and they did.

As soon as the plane landed, my litter was carried to a waiting helicopter. I don't recall the helicopter trip to Tripler Hospital, but I do remember that they were prepared for the worst and had an entire ward reserved just for POWs. But there was only me. When I entered prison, I was in solitary confinement. Now that I was home in the United States I was back in solo. In a fuzzy state of high fever, I pitched a fit.

"How long will I be here before going to Scott?"

They gave a truthful response, "You will be heading home as soon as we get you ready to travel."

"That is no answer; I want to know exactly, I want to see my family."

"Sir, we assure you, it won't be long."

"Okay, get my family here on the next plane."

The doctor said, "That is not a good plan, you will get to Scott soon."

"Soon is not my plan—I want to see my family today. It can't be more than eight hours from Scott to here."

There was more discussion; they would not commit to fly Gaylee and Dawn to Honolulu. I asked them to call "Homecoming Headquarters." To my surprise, in ten minutes I was connected to the Homecoming Command Center. I asked them to put my family on the plane returning from Scott to Hickam. They said they couldn't.

"Why not?"

"Policy" was the curt response.

By now my temperature had stabilized at 101, my body was full of pills and shots, and they declared me fit to fly. Again, to the credit of the Homecoming committee, they had planned for all contingencies. Waiting at Hickam was a C-141 on standby to fly home any POWs who had been held over at Tripler. I was the only passenger.

Just a short helicopter trip to a waiting C-141, and we were on the active runway. I was in a litter again. The only others on board were the crew, a nurse, and flight surgeon. I was feeling sheepish about having my own airliner just hours after ranting and raving about how the Air Force would not fly Gaylee and Dawn to Hawaii.

We had been airborne about three hours when, in the dim cabin lights, I got off the litter and moved around the cavernous cabin. I visited the cockpit. Although this was a four-engine cargo plane, I knew many of the dials, knobs, and flight instruments. The flight crew and I spoke the same language.

I had flown my F-105 Wild Weasel westward toward Vietnam past the Golden Gate Bridge. I recalled now how beautiful San Francisco Bay had seemed to me. I had passed over Alcatraz, and I remembered the fleeting thought the sight of the prison island had triggered: that it was not inconceivable that everyone in my flight could become captives in the fight we were entering.

Now, it was a pitch-black cloudless night over the Pacific. I asked the crew how long before we could see the glow of San Francisco on the horizon. "Less than an hour," the pilot said.

"Would you ask me up here again? I'd like to see the first glimpse."

"You got it, Colonel—happy to do so."

Unknown to me, the crew of Homecoming Seven (our call sign because we were the seventh plane to bring POWs home) had already told San Francisco Center that one POW was on board and that he would be making the position report. Forty minutes later they asked me to come forward. They turned the cockpit lights down. Looking hard, I could see a slight glow off the nose of the aircraft: the ambient lights of the continental United States. I was filled to the full with emotions I couldn't name.

Handing me the mike, the pilot said, "Colonel, our call sign is Homecoming Seven—would you like to make our position report?"

"I'd love to, where are we?"

"Two hundred miles due west of SFO."

It had been a long time, but it seemed natural to be calling an FAA center. "San Francisco Center, this is Homecoming Seven."

"Read you loud and clear, Homecoming Seven."

Before I could answer, the first few bars of "Don't Fence Me In" came in loud and clear over the frequency. Someone said, "Welcome home, we've waited a long time!" With the small composure I had left, I said, "Thank you San Francisco Center, we are 200 miles due west." Their next sentence is still clear in my mind. "Homecoming Seven, be advised you have presidential clearance from your position direct to St. Louis." Speechless, I handed the mike back to the co-pilot.

CHAPTER 22

HOME

Just as I had trouble getting to Scott Air Force Base from Hawaii, Gaylee and Dawn had trouble getting to Scott Air from South Dakota. Just before taking off, the North Central airliner they were on pulled to the far edge of the taxiway and stopped. The captain announced, "Mrs. Thorsness, would you please come to the cabin?" Gaylee's heart skipped a beat as she worked her way up the aisle. (This was 1973, long before 9/11. Cockpit doors were often open until takeoff.) She saw that the captain had turned in his seat waiting for her. "Mrs. Thorsness, because of a high fever your husband is being kept in Hawaii."

"Will he get to Scott sometime tomorrow with the other POWs?"

"We were just told over the radio he will not get to Scott AFB tomorrow."

"How much of a fever does he have?"

The captain, seeing Gaylee was understandably upset, continued calmly, "I tried for more information. They just said it is high but he will be okay."

Gaylee couldn't believe it. So many disappointments over the last six years.

"Mrs. Thorsness, what do you want to do—do you want to go on to Scott or stay in Sioux Falls? I will taxi you back to the terminal if you want to stay here."

"Are you sure you can't find out more about Leo and when he may get to Scott AFB?"

"I just tried, and they have no more information." After a

few seconds of waiting, the understanding captain said, "Mrs. Thorsness, you have waited six years. I will shut the engines down right here, you take your time to decide if you want to go, or stay in Sioux Falls." He added, "Let me know when you decide."

Gaylee hesitated a few seconds, and then said, "Let's go."

Shortly after getting to Scott, Gaylee got a call through to me in the Tripler Hospital in Hawaii. We made frequent calls the next few hours, and, as soon as I knew I was cleared to fly home, I called her.

The next day, March 10, Scott did everything to make a welcome home celebration for one POW as good as the ceremony when all the other POWs arrived the day before. Even in the early morning mist, it was my six-year dream come true.

Gaylee and Dawn were driven in a staff car to the tarmac a few minutes before my C-141 landed. As we came to a stop, looking out the window I could see two beautiful women near the end of the red carpet. One I recognized immediately. How could I forget that face I had thought about every day for six years? The other, at a distance of 150 yards, I did not recognize. "Could that be Dawn?" I asked myself. "It has to be." Would it be right to hug this beautiful young woman?

Gaylee was first to reach me. Then Dawn. As they held me, I felt at last that my life, which had gone to sleep, was awake again.

———

Doctors told me that three surgeries would be required to rebuild my knees and repair my back, but that they would allow me to live mostly pain free and to walk normally. Each day I spent a few hours with our Air Force debriefers. It was long and detailed. Mostly they were looking to find out how we did as POWs. Had we resisted to the best of our ability? They were also looking for any information we had that would prove certain American aviators had gotten out of their aircraft alive, but never showed up in the North Vietnamese prison system.

I had come home into time warp. In an effort to "catch up" with the world, I lay in my hospital bed reading the World Book Encyclopedia year books. I started with the most recent year, 1972, and read backwards. Usually my wife or daughter was with me to answer lots of questions about events in the books. This helped me fill in some of my blanks.

Gaylee's family had worked shoulder to shoulder with her writing letters, putting up billboards, and rallying support to pressure the North Vietnamese to stop torturing us. Gaylee's sisters and their husbands—Lylah and Stan Swanson, Vange and Bob Renshaw—and her mom, Ida, were the POWs' best friends. It was a thrill to see them and to be able to thank them personally just days after my release from Hanoi.

My sister, Donna, brother, John, and mother arrived at Scott two days after Gaylee and Dawn. I had a lot of catching up to do. John was married to Marky, and they had five children. When I left for combat, he was running a garage in Storden, Minnesota. He had decided to be a minister and finished four years of college and Lutheran seminary while I was in prison. As soon as he got to Scott hospital, I asked if he would give me communion. As I took the wafer into my mouth, I thanked God once again for having brought me home to this country, these people, and this life.